Color Your Message

Getting people to understand the tremendous opportunities to improve your business branding and marketing led me to create "**Color Your Message**!"

Having had hundreds of conversations and interviews about business over the past several years, I found that there is a disconnect between people who have been in business over twenty years and the younger generation on how they receive their messages.

Many older business people who are experts in their field do not understand the social media components or understand what to do. Until just a few short years, ago your business could survive with basic marketing, as simple as black and white. And then almost overnight everything changed with high-speed Internet and mobile devices that could deliver the world. Business marketing exploded into a full palette of colors.

Learn how to jump start your messages and branding today.

COLOR YOUR MESSAGE

THE ART OF DIGITAL MARKETING AND SOCIAL MEDIA

#1 Best Seller

By Lisa Caprelli

COLOR

YOUR

MESSAGE

THE ART OF DIGITAL MARKETING
AND SOCIAL MEDIA

LISA CAPRELLI

DEDICATION

To my wonderful sons, Matthew and Trey, you inspire me to do more and be more. Being a mother is one of the greatest joys of my life! Matthew is so talented and a gift from God. Trey is a determined sports-driven bundle of pure boy energy. They are both forces of nature. Your kids are, after all, a reflection of yourself for others to enjoy.

To my beautiful partner, Brian. You changed my life and helped me through worlds of struggle by bringing love and family back into our lives.

To my siblings who love me no matter what: Debbie, Suzanne, Ruth, and Mike. Special thanks to Alyssa Ortiz, an excellent writer and Millennial who helps us see things with a creative perspective.

To my mother, Esperanza, who deserves more credit for raising five children on her own. I get it now.

To my Tia Lucy, an amazing soul. To my close friends and loved ones who have become engrained in my heart. And to a special friend that once said, "You matter to so many." Thank you all for believing in me and supporting me through the years.

To my Grandma, you are the essence of love. You are in our words and roots. My eyes see the same views and gaiety you saw. You are grace and humility. You are loved by so many! Your home is always my castle.

"The role of a creative leader is not to have all the ideas; it's to create a culture where everyone can have ideas and feel that they're valued."
-Ken Robinson

CONTENTS

"If you are working on something exciting that you really care about, you don't have to be pushed. The vision pulls you."
-Steve Jobs

ACKNOWLEDGMENTS

This book could not have happened without the contributions and wealth of information of many fine people including Google, Pew Research and LinkedIn Influencers. Thanks to the readers, colleagues, and friends I've been privileged to know over the years.

Do not underestimate the power of the simple act of believing in someone – one never knows what triggers another to do great things. It took the action of just one person believing in me to remain motivated throughout my youth. My wonderful and loving grandmother did just that. She is one of the few people in my childhood that gave me, a super shy girl, encouragement, recognition, and praise.

My dad left my mom with five children to raise on her own when I was four. Grandma returned to work at a school cafeteria to help my mother and reduce the hardship. We were welfare kids. She always said, over and over, "Get an education, that is the best thing you can do for yourself." And we did.

Perception is everything, isn't it?

I remember Grandma's house being like a castle to me. It was so full of love and good energy. If you have never known what that is like, it is

the richest feeling on earth. Laughter and love filled our lives. We knew one day we would grow up and our lives would change. You cannot ever know what love and connection is like unless you have truly had or felt it.

Grandma's house was nothing close to a castle, yet every morning she would look outside her kitchen window as if she were seeing something beautiful. The awe in her eyes made me dream of the awe I would feel one day looking out the window of my own house. In reality, what was outside her window was an ugly house, as the true beauty laid far beyond.

When I return to her home in Texas, I think to myself, "Wow, this house is very small. What was I seeing back then?" I was taking in her perception and the love with which she filled the room. I can still visualize those days in my head and the deep-rooted memories of Grandma, a strong, matriarchal woman who believed in a little girl and loved so many! I love giving to others what Grandma gave to me. This is why I get so passionate as I am privileged to help you live to your full potential, believe in you, motivate you, and guide you, when given the opportunity.

ABOUT THE AUTHOR

With a 10 year radio career overlapping 19 years in consulting, marketing, branding and growing companies, Lisa Caprelli uses content and message branding in a 360 degree strategy.

After many years of putting off her final three college courses, she completed her degree in May 2014 and graduated magna cum laude (4.0 GPA) with a Bachelor of Science in Social Psychology from Park University.

Over the years, Lisa has become widely known as a source of inspiring others to take action with their growth and business innovation. She has helped CEO's run businesses since she was 19. She has worked with Fortune 500 companies. At 21, Lisa became a court reporter (reading and writing 250 words per minute). She got an early start spearheading her gift to help others succeed with creative marketing ideas, innovation, and implementation. At age 29 she moved from Texas to Orange County, California to begin working on her own business dreams. Within a year, Lisa had co-founded, directed, and marketed a successful business through effective media and PR campaigns.

"I CAN DO THINGS YOU CANNOT, YOU CAN DO THINGS I CANNOT; TOGETHER WE CAN DO GREAT THINGS." -MOTHER TERESA

Lisa began developing an array of marketing tools, team-building, relationships, referrals and systems. Now she is proud to share her written works as well as find the "niche" within you that people want to read and hear about. After hosting the mortgage real estate radio show (*The Solomon Free Money Hour* with Kerri Kasem), Lisa went on to host *The Business Experience Show* on KLAA AM830, heavily promoted through blogs, social media and video channels.

Her media career has included a mortgage radio show, real estate finance books, business marketing shows, motivational books, and radio productions on stations like 97.1 FM, KFWB, KNX 1070, KFMB, and KABC. Today she combines traditional with digital media to enhance public relations, content marketing, and brand messaging with an outside-the-box approach. Utilizing digital journalism, public relations, social media, marketing, and advertising, Lisa Caprelli collaborates with like-minded CEO's, business owners & entrepreneurs.

Today Lisa teaches you how to market your business on a reasonable budget.

"I love what I do and the best part is working with awesome and influential people! Taking the time to balance life and enjoy family is important! Being a mother is one of my greatest joys.

Affiliations:	OC Public Relations Society of America
Twitter:	@BusinessExpShow @GoGlossy
Instagram:	GoGlossy
Hashtag:	#ColorYourMessage
Email:	PR@GoGlossy.com

FOREWORD

There is no more "business as usual." How we do business today is changing at a remarkable pace. Are you keeping up?

While the fundamentals of a good business model are still consistent, it is the marketing and communication that has changed at unparalleled rates. New tools, techniques, and methods that did not exist just a few short years ago are now commonplace for the strategic and ambitious marketer. Traditional marketing has been supplemented with dynamic social media marketing. Social media requires all of us who *serve customers*, to do business differently, whether your business is big or small, public or private, service or product-based.

How we communicate with our customers and future customers is fluid and relational. We moved into an era of mass-customization and personalization. You must know and keep up with these modern changes. Since the marketplace is simultaneously both local and global, your message can not afford to get lost among the crowd. What is your message and how are you differentiating yourself? That is where this book can help you.

Established businesses are losing market share to younger businesses that are more effectively using these new tools. If your business is not putting forth a maximum effort in reaching rapidly mobile and Internet-informed customers, then you are losing out on market share.

While the most effective marketing uses of social media are often debated, a basic understanding of each of the major outlets is necessary. This book is a toolkit that explains the digital business marketing landscape in terms we can all understand.

Jumpstart your marketing program today to help ensure your success tomorrow.

Stephen Christensen
Dean, School of Business
Concordia University Irvine
#Teen4Biz

"I never lose. I either win or I learn."
~Anonymous

CHAPTER 1:
What Color Is Your Message?

Some see their ideas as creative and act on their creative flair. I was no exception when I woke up with the idea that started with a question: *What Color Is Your Message?* We have had hundreds of conversations and interviews about people and their business over the past several years and found that there is a disconnect between people who have been in business over twenty years and the younger generation on how they receive their messages. Many older business people who are experts in their field do not understand the social media components or understand what to do. Until just a few short years ago your business could survive with basic marketing, as simple as black and white. And then almost overnight everything changed with high-speed Internet and mobile devices that could deliver the world. Business marketing exploded into a full palette of colors.

Black and White

We used to live in a society where it mattered if you had been a business owner for over 20 years. It used to be credible if you were in business even 30 or 40 years. Employees loved to say they worked with a company for decades. Employers used to tout their long term existence with seals of approval. I feel that today, most people simply care about their bottom line cost and to some extent how they are found online. If you are not fully utilizing today's technology and tools you may get lost completely.

92% of Americans have some online presence by the age of 2, think about it, and think about your children and grandchildren.

Visualize colors representing marketing elements: one color is Facebook, one color is LinkedIn, one color is Twitter and yet another is your message. Imagine your world of potential customers as a black and white coloring book of millions of people. This is where we are today. There are so many tools, and instead of being overwhelmed by them, start using a few of them in your business or hire someone who knows what they are doing. Let us take out colors and start coloring your message to reach your potential audience!

What Color Is Your Message?

One of the big problems is that the change in the economy paralleled the shift in the importance of social media for businesses and online marketing. A lot of people were fighting with the financial struggle and they did not catch that shift. They missed it completely. Many businesses today are still outdated with their marketing. It is not up to speed and they are still saying *it is the economy, my business is slow*, when in fact, the economy has picked up.

This is the new economy. This is it. And it is also the new marketing. When we hear people blame their lack of business on the economy and then we take a look at their marketing, it is not anywhere close to where it needs to be. There are businesses that are starting every day. We meet new business owners and they are doing well because they have an understanding of what they need to be doing in today's market place and they are doing it. It is typically the older businesses that were stymied by the faltering economy and they miss the new marketing component completely. Marketing today is completely different than it was five years ago.

It is an exciting time to be a business expert and realize your business can grow by implementing the right strategies and action steps! You can connect with anyone around the world with a shared interest using today's technology.

Getting the right people on the bus; the wrong people off the bus are *Good to Great* traits, along with: humility, strong drive, known for taking blame for bad decisions and **giving credit for good ones!** *Going understaffed for a while is better than having a bad team.*

GOOD TO GREAT: Why Some Companies Make the Leap and Others Don't Great insight by author, Jim Collins

#ColorYourMessage

This is my simple question to you: **"If I gave you a free radio ad, would you use it for your business?"**

"Yes," is the common reply. Well, that is what social media and all the digital tools available today are the equivalent of -- *today*!"

I spent over a million dollars in the early 2000's on radio advertising that had a favorable return on our marketing investment. However, with digital tools and technology available today, I often find myself not even considering radio as a form of advertising for my customers. There are so many other free and inexpensive tools that are way more powerful.

You do not have to be Richard Branson or Emeril Lagasse to be a brand, each of you has your own reputation and expertise to show off and by expressing who you are as individuals, you can create relationships with potential customers.

A third of all online activity is spent watching videos. YouTube is considered the number two search engine in the world. Video traffic is expected to grow to 78% by 2018 to comprise the bulk of online traffic. If your company does not have a set video strategy in place, then you should take action now!

If you think you can simply refuse to participate in digital marketing for your business, you should know that your online identity is being created whether you participate in it or not. If you are a business and saying, "Oh, I don't need this, I just want to stick with black and white messaging, I don't want to do all this digital stuff" think about this. Your customers are creating your content. They are reviewing you online. They are talking about you in social circles. You need to be involved in it you need to help shape your content.

People ask, "What other tools should businesses be using, what should we be doing?" You should be looking at what the conversations about you and your business are online. Join those conversations. Help shape

What Color Is Your Message?

them and address positive or negative reviews. Get involved. Roll up your sleeves and participate.

Take 30 seconds to catch you up on business marketing today versus the thinking of yesteryear.

20th Century	21st Century
Word Of Mouth	Social Media
Personal Recommendations	Social Media, Photo Sharing Sites
Professional Credentials	Linked In Profile
Radio Advertising	Video SEO
Newspaper/Magazine Advertising	Blog Posts About Your Business
Yellow Page Listing	Keyword Marketing
Yellow Page Advertisement	Pay Per Click Ads
Creating A Buzz	Mass Sharing and Likes
Direct Marketing	Online Searches Finding Your Business (SEO)

The Tough Reality

Unfortunately, the growth and importance of online marketing was paralleled by the economic recession of the past several years. This created an environment in which the true impact of the dramatic shift in consumer marketing went unnoticed.

- What is your reason for your business existing – beyond making money?
- Can you answer the question *why does your business exist*?
- Are you getting found online? Google's search engine is used by 85% of Internet users every month.
- Do you have an effective and strong web presence?
- Have you used a little bit of social media or no social media because you just do not understand it completely?
- Social media is not going away.
- The ways people find your business keywords are changing and expanding every day.
- If you are not getting found your competition is.

- If you are one of those who still thinks a bad economy is hurting your business, you need to think again.

- A bad economy is no longer to blame – it is your outdated marketing, lack of innovation, or weak web presence.
- There is a great techno-logical divide between the baby boomer genera-tion and the Millennials. (See CHAPTER 8: Statistics & Data)
- Instead of avoiding your business advertising and doing nothing, embrace it and learn how to take advantage of the oppor-tunities – many of them FREE – that exist all around you.

Ironic! She never believed in advertising her business, yet today she is advertising her going out of business sale.

The importance of using digital media to effectively REACH your potential NEW customers and ENGAGE your EXISTING customers is critical. Word of mouth is no longer ear-to-ear, but at the reach of a fingertip. And if you wait much longer, it might be out of reach.

Surprisingly, many business owners still do not understand the value of investing in online branding. Your digital presence is far more important as a whole than just social media, which is a sub-category. An improper message can hurt your brand more than no message at all. Online branding is crucial to your customers finding you today and beyond. Be sure you are taking an active role in creating it for your business.

The algorithms that drive Search Engine Optimization change so rapidly that if you are not participating in a comprehensive online strategy, your SEO can be here today, gone tomorrow.

What Color Is Your Message?

How all successful businesses should operate experienced a tipping point in 2009 and forever changed the landscape, especially evident today. There is a generational, cultural and socio economic divide that needs to be addressed in your business marketing. Diversity is now commonplace. I invite you to learn how you can be part of your own solution, as well as create a meaningful work and life in order to leave a legacy and business you can one day sell or pass on to your family.

Do not feel bad if you do not get this aspect of marketing, you are not alone. I went to a Hollywood screening of a movie and at the very end there was a Q&A for the audience. I raised my hand and said "Your movie was well made and you can see you have a big audience here willing to follow and support where you take it next. What are your social media handles or hashtags?" The director laughed and hesitantly replied, "Um, I still have a pager." Here is an expert dealing with a multi-million dollar movie budget!

I am shocked at the generational divide. Through understanding, one can grow and then make the choice and decisions to become better.

> *Greatness is not a function of circumstances. Greatness, it turns out, is largely a matter of conscious choice and discipline. – Jim Collins, Author of <u>Good to Great: Why Some Companies Make the Leap and Others Don't</u>*

CHAPTER 2:
Dreams Bigger Than Texas

I came to California in 2001 with nothing but a hundred dollars in my bank account, dreams bigger than my Texas hairdo, huge enthusiasm, and little fear of what "no" would mean. Everyone told me I was not going to make it. Crazy as it was, all these years later I laugh when I look back. *Yes that was me.*

I spent most of my twenties working on building businesses, rising to the top, becoming director of marketing for this company, right hand to the CEO of that company, superstar worker for another. Growing up a straight-A student and an extreme introvert, I have to tell you I learned that the rich certainly do get richer. Having straight A's does not mean anything when you go to the workforce. Your voice, how you speak, who you know, and how well you understand and approach business seems to be how people will notice you more.

> *"Passion, not pedigree, will win in the end." – Jon Bon Jovi*

When you work in an hourly position, you work your butt off with little compensation in return. I recall one of my first employers saying, "It's such cheap labor here in El Paso." He was a Caucasian businessman and I was a Hispanic young worker in the city of El Paso, Texas bordering Juarez, Mexico. It is a border town of predominantly Hispanic culture.

Dreams Bigger Than Texas

Telling you I grew up very poor will not matter. There are always poorer out there that are more poor than you. I often felt like I was born in the wrong place. Not the wrong family. I love my family and upbringing. I mean how do you know you are poor until someone else tells you? Little things like having ice cream in your freezer or having curtains on your window, to me, meant you were rich.

I cannot even tell you how many times I was told "no."

Each answer was, "No, we don't have the money" for things:
- *Can I have ten cents for popcorn at lunchtime?*
- *Everyone makes fun of me at school. Can I have nicer glasses instead of these thick ones?*
- *Can I have a birthday party?*
- *Can I have new socks, these are torn?*
- *Mom, can I buy this book from school, everyone is getting one?*
- *Can I –*
- *No, Lisa!*

After a while you stop asking. You just know that the answer is *No*. *No* is not a fun answer. It is one of rejection. *No* shuts you down. I hate *No*.

> *Never allow a person to tell you no who doesn't have the power to say yes. – Eleanor Roosevelt*

Have you ever known a little boy who just loves to take things apart? Maybe you were one of those…things disassembled, parts laying everywhere…just to see how things work.

Well, I was never a boy. And I do not really use wrenches, but I have always been like that about marketing. I can remember at a very young age trying to understand why some messages worked better than others.

I would make it my mission to find the best way to get my message through to understand how things work, to understand the world, and to help others.

This could be part of being the middle child in a large Hispanic family. My interest or drive to help others inspired me to pursue a degree in Social Psychology.

> *If one does not understand a person, one tends to regard him as a fool – CG Jung*

Who's Fooling Who?

At 8 years old, I started paying attention to marketing and messages. I used to subscribe to free mail offers just to see the advertising. I listened to radio ads and carefully read the Penny Saver, coupons, billboards, and cereal boxes. When we finally got a television at age 10, I began observing television commercials and what made them influential.

Essentially, we are being sold something our whole life. We are being marketed to all the time. We just learn to tune out what does not matter to us.

I love the word "marketing." I love its beautiful power of persuasion. It is the process of using communication to convey the value of a product or service.

Value denotes usefulness. And who does not want to be or feel useful? It is an innate human function.

If you translate value into your business or personal life, I promise you it can be exponential beyond your wildest dreams.

I love the value of committing to turn someone's business around or make it significantly better. If you make someone rich, they are going to be your good friend.

Friends say yes. Remember, I do not like the word no.

Dreams Bigger Than Texas

Today, I rarely will set myself up for a question where I am told no.

I realized the power in achieving the opposite of *no* meant doing things for other people and resulted in "yes, Lisa."

Would you like me to clean your yard and pay me what you want?

Would you like to buy a lollipop for my fundraiser?

I would skate around for hours selling a five cent lollipop for ten cents. Double my profits. I realized being geeky paid off. For one, I started getting a hundred yeses. I knew that once I turned 17, my life could be full of yeses and with that I started my own plans to figure out how to turn my life around. With little guidance and not far to fall, those experiences turned me into the tough business woman I am today. I have no regrets.

> *It may sound strange, but many champions are made champions by setbacks. – Bob Richards*

The Power Of Struggle

There was something about California I found irresistible: sun-infused energy, synergy, and an entrepreneurial spirit. Let us not forget it is a place of possibility, a place where "yes" resided.

I told people that I came here with a smile. Many seemed to appreciate that candor and vulnerability. Not one person in my family or friends supported my decision to move to California. I was told things like:
- *Why would you want to leave your family?*
- *You won't make it.*
- *California has lots of drugs.*
- *What makes you think you'll survive?*
- *It's tough to make it. You'll be back.*

One of your best characteristics as a human being can be to support and believe in your fellow man. I have built startups based on believing in the value of offering customers something that no one else can. Your passion, your desire to make something, is more than just a dream. It is something you can do. And with the right team, anything is possible. Likewise, I remain vulnerable and open to new possibilities. There is always someone who knows more than you. You can always learn from others.

In fact, when competing for new business in an unfamiliar industry a company will invariably ask why they should work with my company which has no previous experience in their industry. My quick response is that my naivety about their business will benefit them when I begin to look at their marketing with an outsider's point of view, much like many of their customers view it.

Taking risks is essentially what has driven the most successful people. Urgency creates movement, which makes for action. Take the leap of faith in yourself and start your vision, your plan. Do not try to wait until your plan is 100% organized and perfect. It will never be! If you just go, society will help you and tell you where your flaws are and you can adjust. Once you are going you create urgency for yourself. Once urgency comes into play, fear is removed. I had an urgent mission: get to California, become an entrepreneur, do not look back. I have failed from some of my risks, but have benefitted from most of them. Life is change. Life is about risk. "How will I ever know if it's the right or wrong thing if I never do it?" That was my common reply to the naysayers.

The support from complete strangers in Orange County, California was enormous. People actually liked my $100 story and the enthusiasm and vulnerability I had to make anything possible.

Struggle is a word I embrace daily in my vocabulary. I love movies like *The Blind Side* and *Forrest Gump* and movies that have a challenge to overcome. If you do not know you cannot do something, then essentially it is your perception that limits you. You can become

Dreams Bigger Than Texas

or be anyone you want to be. "I strive to teach my children that there will always be struggles in life, but so long as you embrace the great moments and prepare for the worst moments, change will never take you by surprise." Struggle does bring benefit.

Sports are a perfect example of teams experiencing struggle and turning that into a winning quality. The victory can be measured by the score, individual achievement, or emotional triumph.

> *"Sports remain a great metaphor for life's more difficult lessons. It was through athletics that many of us first came to understand that fear can be tamed; that on a team the whole is more than the sum of its parts; and that the ability to be heroic lies, to a surprising degree, within."* – Susan Casey

"Why did you move here?" was asked every time I said that I moved from Texas. The real answer was, "Because I could."

You can do anything you set your mind and actions to do!

I am here to tell you that I could not have made it were it not for the people I relied on, who graciously helped make California a beautiful home for the years to come.

> *Every day is a new opportunity. You can build on yesterday's success or put its failures behind and start over again. That's the way life is, with a new game every day, and that's the way baseball is.* – Bob Feller

In 2002, I partnered with a mortgage broker, took a year's worth of savings, and put everything into marketing. I invested it all in radio advertising. I knew I could use my marketing skills and take on the competition head-on without fear.

What is your competitive edge?

Every business should identify one. Do not be afraid of competition. Embrace it.

With my new mortgage company a strong work ethic, purposeful commitment, and doing the right thing for others was going to pay off. And it did. In 2003 we were ranked as one of the top 5 mortgage companies in Orange County for volume. We continued to rank high year after year.

I had my own business and for the first time was not working for someone else. The amount of money we made in one month was more than I could have imagined. It previously would have taken me five years to make what we were making in one month; it was amazing. I was on cloud nine for years.

We were able to go on vacations I could have only dreamed of before. We had money to buy real estate in a variety of places including Kauai, Hawaii. Growing up I only got to see the ocean on television. I remember watching *Fantasy Island* and seeing visions of the beautiful blue waters of a tropical island. It seemed like a place you could visit only if you were lucky enough to have those opportunities or have a family that had money to vacation like that. Many of my years in California have been like a vacation to me. I have said, "Oh, my gosh," more than you can imagine. The number of times I was told "no" in my youth has now been outnumbered by "yes." There is so much beauty, wonder, and great places in the world to see. Now I get to share these experiences with my family and remind them how fortunate they are to see things I never thought possible.

We bought a Dodge Viper, Ferrari 360, Spyder, BMW 850i, and Jaguar. My partner at the time was a car enthusiast. I am not a flashy person and am happy driving my Toyota Prius present day.

Fast forward to 2008, 2009 – recession time!

As if the universe was not giving me enough with having to leave my marriage, the economy decided to plummet. No more struggle, please. I did not need more beneficial life lessons at this time.

Dreams Bigger Than Texas

Businesses were changing and so were we. Starting over again in the coming years seemed like more of a struggle than when I moved in 2001 with nothing. I felt alone. It was the most arduous thing I have ever experienced. Putting your soul into a business and working 60 hours a week year after year to come to the realization that you have to start over is indescribable. *Beyond being a labor of Sisyphus, it felt like abuse, betrayal, and injustice.*

It felt like I had no one to understand the insurmountable pain that would come. In fact, I tried seeking local meet up groups using keywords on Google such as: "How to start over after leaving your business partner" with additional keywords "whom you married." When one door closes, another door opens.

It was mountains of struggle, loss, and perseverance to rebuild and rebrand. I did it one step at a time, making many mistakes, figuring out my brand, and learning who I was. How could I help the world? I knew that if I gave up, all this would have been for nothing. The epiphany was to not give up. Keep moving. Yes, there was a mountain of struggle and another, and yet another, but the climbing does eventually bring you to the end. The end being the result. The result starts with purpose.

> *Many persons have a wrong idea of what constitutes true happiness. It is not attained through self-gratification but through fidelity to a worthy purpose.* – Helen Keller

Purpose was an aspect in almost every part of this new mission. I found it helpful to go back to the basics and find purpose. I would rely on, "What is your purpose?" to be a question I would ask others around me, especially business men and women. Do not lose sight of your purpose.

Even though I ran a real estate mortgage business and we were ethical with our customers and practices, it was not a fun and entirely purposeful business. It was a very stressful and demanding job. I ran the office, created systems, managed staff, built teams and employed marketing strategies that worked. At the end of the day we were just a number. We helped people save money which is a good thing, but it was not utilizing the gifts of helping others that I have been given. Today, when I help any professional, I make sure that your purpose component is identified.

This is what brought me to start my own marketing agency and create this book as a resource for businesses. Bringing purpose to so many people like you is worth the struggle and passion. How rewarding that I get to create and share this knowledge.

Over the years, I have been privileged to interview and work with CEO's of varied industries, magazines, bloggers, restaurants, retailers, celebrities, attorneys, dentists, car dealerships, authors, celebrities, actors, musicians, oil and land men, mortgage, real estate, retail stores, designers and more.

If I had been afraid of struggle, oh, how the cards would have been played differently. I would not have been able to develop the great relationships and help so many people. I am on a mission to help you grow your business. Especially if you are an expert in your field. If you have been in business 20 years or more, I am so glad I found you! You may be missing out on more future business, being found and having purpose. I want to help light that fire within you!

Dreams Bigger Than Texas

It is time to take action. I am going to give you a lot of my secrets and years of research, data and points for you to apply into your business life. If any of this information gets too overwhelming, find someone who understands marketing to help you! Marketing is an *investment* in your purpose and should never be viewed as an expense. If you treated marketing dollars like investment dollars, you would be more inclined to have a professional manage the investment since you know they have more experience and a better chance of having a profitable outcome.

We try never to forget that medicine is for the people. It is not for the profits. The profits follow, and if we have remembered that, they have never failed to appear. The better we have remembered it, the larger they have been. – George Merck, who in 1929 became President of his father's Merck chemical manufacturing company

(Merck's research yielded the first synthesis of vitamins and the first American-made penicillin.)

CHAPTER 3:
The Tipping Point

There are black and white tools coming into play again.

It is important to understand modern technology and tools "available." Prior to 2009, recall how the ways of promoting your business varied from today. Then came the tipping point when the interaction between technology and how you were found online changed drastically. An online web presence became more important than ever. Simply having a website was not enough. How new customers found you became more important than ever. Enter social media, apps, online search engines, and the ever changing algorithms of Google. It was enough to overwhelm most anyone.

Black & White Era

I refer to 2009 as the tipping point where marketing and getting found online – via computer Internet, search, or mobile devices - changed business forever. In a box of many crayons, think of the black and white representing marketing and the tools available pre-2009. The choices we had to promote a business were limited compared to today. I refer to this as the black and white marketing era.

- Radio
- Newsletters
- Yellow Pages
- Mail Coupons
- Magazines
- Billboards
- Direct mail

Think of the colors remaining in the same box of crayons as tools you can use for your business needs.

The Tipping Point

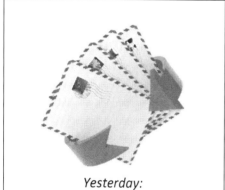

Yesterday:
You sent a letter

Today:
To send a letter means e-mail it

Television Then:
"What will we watch next?"

Television Now:
"I'm watching what I want to."

Colors = Tools

Let us add the other colors back into your business, as if choosing from a box of crayons! It can seem so overwhelming. Where do you start? Changing one's perception can be a challenge unless you are given a vision along with supporting data.

Here we apply *black and white thinking* about some of today's popular digital marketing tools:

- *Facebook*
  It takes a lot of your time.
- *Instagram*
  Isn't Pinterest the same thing?
- *Social Media Person*
  I do not even know what you do.
- *Hashtag*
  I do not know what you are.
- *Twitter*
  How does a tweet get me noticed?
- *SnapChat*
  This message will self-destruct...
- *LinkedIn®*
  I already use Facebook.

The Tipping Point

Now, let's change the perception by looking at those same tools as marketing colors. Here is what you could be saying:

- *Facebook*
  ~~It takes a lot of your time.~~
  My customers become brand ambassadors!
- *Instagram*
  ~~Isn't Pinterest the same thing?~~
  That's how I can reach the 20-something crowd!
- *Social Media Person*
  ~~I do not even know what you do.~~
  You ☺ can help me compile all my content!
- *Hashtag*
  ~~I do not know what you are.~~
  I can target niche marketing segments!
- *Twitter*
  ~~How does a tweet get me noticed?~~
  I can easily promote something or get found via my network!
- *SnapChat*
  ~~This message will self destruct....~~
  Better use the latest wave creating quick *journal videos*!
- *LinkedIn*®
  ~~I already use Facebook.~~
  Great for professional connections and strategic partnerships!

Imagine what the world would be like with only black & white. I encourage you to use these colors, but learn what is right for YOU and realize it is a process.

Digital Media is prevalent today. It is *anything that can be viewed on a screen*:

- E-mails
- Websites
- Videos
- Apps
- Tablets (iPads)
- Social Networks

There are people that speak the social media language extensively. They love sharing their messages on Instagram, Twitter, and Facebook. If you can speak to them on their platform, you are much more likely to build a bond with them. By speaking someone's language you are able to be friends within a shared community. By sharing a connection, this can likely to lead to attention and business. It is like learning another language. You do not have to speak another language, but if you learn to engage in this technology, you will open yourself up to many more possibilities.

Not Tweeting? You May Be Missing Out Professionally

If you are a CEO or president and not on Twitter, you may be missing out on what your employees are saying about your brand, business and more. Why? Because companies are already being talked about on Twitter. Not being there, not listening, not seeing, and not responding for the company or foundation that you direct is being absent and neglecting a great part of the conversation around and about you.

Remain innovative and humble with your associates and colleagues. Show that not only can you direct a company, you also tweet! Why not install the simple APP on your phone or computer? It's FREE! Ask someone to teach you how to use it and show your clients, employees, and friends that you are a real person with humanistic interests, opinions, hobbies, a sense of humor, and so on. People are interested in what it is like being you. They want to know what is going on with your company, your community standpoint. They want to know what is going on with you. Now there are times where you will want to keep certain things about yourself private. Yet, there are times that you will want to share on Twitter notable moments and interactions you have on a weekly or daily basis.

Met someone really cool lately? It's not bragging if you tweet. People will admire you for sharing part of your life that makes you seem like a real human being – not just a stuffy business owner.

You can constantly keep updated on the happenings in your fields of interest and "follow" other brands of information – known as short "tweets" that happen all around you.

You can retweet articles and information you find interesting, creating an ecosystem of people with similar interests. In the old days you would clip out a magazine article and post it on your company bulletin board. Today, technology has changed the way we grab pieces of information.

Once you build a Twitter following, you can engage in debates and actively participate in conversations. It is up to you to decide how you want to use Twitter. However, I recommend that you understand and use it.

Among millennials, those aged 18-34, Snapchat is now the third most popular social media app by smartphone penetration, with 32.9% of that demographic having the friendly ghost on the yellow background floating on their screen. That puts it just behind Instagram (43.1%) and of course Facebook (75.6%)

(Source: http://www.socialmediafrontiers.com/2014/08/snapchat-closing-in-on-established.html)

> *"Learning another language is not only learning different words for the same things, but learning another way to think about things." – Flora Lewis*

CHAPTER 4:
360 Degrees

This 360 degrees graphic shows some of the many elements of digital marketing. If you look closely you will see that the *color* of social media is just *one* element. If you are not using marketing as an "umbrella" that encompasses all of the elements that come underneath it (content writing, branding, video, a modern website, social media, etc.) you are missing out. Think of each circle as a color and the element you should be using in your business. If you have a team of people, delegate colors to them and outsource the colors you do not know or are costing you too much time. Do not be afraid to pay for that, because if you do it properly you are going to get a significant return on investment and increase in business.

#SocialMedia
#DontBeABusinessDinosuar
#YourCatchPhrase

A restaurant owner once told me, "Yeah, I am doing marketing. I have someone doing my *social media* for me." Well, I was inspired to create this graphic for you.

My reply was, "So you are telling me that you only do one of these circles? Let me guess, you are not seeing results from your marketing, right?"

"You are right, Lisa. How did you know?"

There are many elements that go into a strategic marketing plan that can benefit full circle for you under the umbrella of *marketing*. Sure, you can use just one color, but based on experience, I would not want to be part of that kind of plan.

Greatness Doesn't Sell -- Marketing Does

Too often I hear "My idea is worth a million dollars!" "Um, no it is not. Your idea is worth zero dollars. The execution of a great idea and strategic plan is what brings value to any business.

> Author and marketer, Edwin Dearborn says, "The idea that your great idea or product will sell due to its inherent merits and value is why 50% of businesses in America fail in the first 18 months and 90% within 5 years. These business people get so sold on their own hype, ego and importance, that they forget the most important element in business and marketing: The Customer! That customer could not care less about your bottom line, your problems or how awesome you are at what you do. Your education level, experience or how great your golf game is means absolutely nothing to customers–really. They care only about themselves, not you, and that's the way it is. If you don't know what that potential customer truly thinks, feels, wants and even demands, then you won't hit the ball out of the park. And all those facets of your customer change rapidly and continually."

Marketing Is Not An "Expense" It Is An Investment

If you view marketing as an expense – you have got it all wrong! I have seen this time and time again. I could not have started any business I ever had without "marketing dollars." Look at your business like a "fix and flip" piece of property. It could be real estate investor's dream to buy a $30,000 *fix & flip*, turn it around, and sell it for 10 times its purchase price. Before you can create this kind of value, you would have to renovate it, stage it, make it beautiful and then turn around and sell it for its marketable value. The investor does not make money when it is bought at $30,000 – the investor only makes a significant return when she invests in the property, markets it properly, and sells it at a lucrative price. The same analogy holds true for marketing your business.

@EdwinDearborn goes on to say: Marketing is the necessary and vital business process of creating desire and moving products and/or services into the hands of consumers. Only marketing can create desire and thus move massive amounts of product into the hands of eager buyers. It is a grave mistake to categorize marketing as merely an "expense." By assuming that viewpoint, many businesses abruptly halt the small business marketing strategies that could very well move them forward and upward, all for the sake of "cutting expenses."

Unfortunately, too many business people tend to cut their marketing budgets in a knee-jerk reaction when they encounter financial strain. Yet, cutting back on your marketing efforts is the last thing you should be doing.

Well-executed and intelligent promotion is your best path out of financial stress. Market research has proven conclusively that those companies that increase marketing efforts during hard times expand far in excess of their competitors when the economy eventually takes an upswing.

Marketing begins with research and a well thought out plan.

You Get What You Pay For

This well-worn adage has a place when it comes to budgeting for your marketing expenses. The salary of a good marketing account executive should be upward of $75,000 annually. While outsourcing your needs to a part-time consultant should cost significantly less, I consistently run into business owners, struggling with their marketing strategies, who tell me that their monthly marketing budget is $500 or less. Think about it…that is the equivalent of a $6,000 per year employee. And if you find a company willing to take your account for that amount, then you are by all means likely to get exactly what you pay for.

Tools To Ponder

Video
Creating and editing your video.
What type of video should you create?
Should it be hosted on your website or YouTube?
(see CHAPTER 17: Video)

Website
Do you need a modernized website?
When was the last time you made updates to your website?
Does it include social media icons?
Does it have a blog included in it?

SEO (Search Engine Optimization)
Are your business keywords branded?
Are you found on the top search engine pages organically?
Are you locked into pay per click ads?
You can break the cycle.

Social Media
There are many social media sites such as Facebook, Twitter, LinkedIn, Instagram, Pinterest, Vine, Tumblr, Flickr.
How are you utilizing them and which ones should you use?

Branding
Is your logo and brand consistent across the platforms listed above?
Should they be?
Do you have one name for one social media site and then another for a different site?
Do you have an easily recognizable logo or is it merely your name in a special font?

Google and YouTube
Is your business properly listed on Google?
Do you show up in the search results for YouTube?
These platforms are the most popular domestic search engines and they are FREE.
Is your business professionally represented in all of the appropriate areas?

Content
What are the messages you are promoting?
What are your clients saying about you across the board?

All of these tools help your business have an impact through better visibility. They can help you get more website traffic and convert traffic to dollars.

Each colored circle represents a different component in your business. There are many tools not listed, such as:

- E-mail marketing
- Radio advertising
- Television ads
- Banner ads
- Contests and promotions
- Traditional note cards
- Referrals
- Business directories
- Apps
- Review sites
- Direct marketing campaigns
- Employee customer interaction
- And much, much more!

Yet in the 360 degree circle, these elements will cross over and be necessary to work together to drive more traffic to your website, social media, and your online web presence.

Blaming It All On Social Media

Remember, you can avoid a common mistake by visualizing social media as just *one* piece to the 360 overview. There are MANY elements to marketing that all start with a proper message.

Seven Ways to Improve Your Website

When someone clicks on your home page, what they immediately see influences 90% of their decisions – leave or stay on your website.

If you want to promote a business in today's world, the best way to do it is to get found online. There is not a day that goes by that I do not hear someone say, "Google it!"

Setting up a website can be a great and inexpensive way to reach new clients, generate leads, and improve conversion rates for your product or service. When it comes to designing a website, your focus should be on providing value for your visitors. This will make people want to come back to your site and learn more about what you're saying.

Here are seven tips for improving your website to increase traffic and improve conversion rates.

1. Your logo

When it comes to website design, the old adage is true: *you only get one chance to make a first impression.* Your website is the first thing about your business that your web visitors will encounter. Your official business logo is the first indicator that visitor's usually look at to judge the quality of a site and the professionalism of the business. Try to avoid using free themes and logos, as this can make your website look and feel generic. If you can't afford the services of a professional graphic artist to create original designs, consider outsourced sites, where creative professionals offer their services as a low-cost "gig." There are pros and cons to "looking cheap," so be sure you pick what is right for your brand.

2. Relevant Content

In order to attract and keep visitors on your site, you need to provide fresh, relevant content. Your web pages need to engage the reader, not offer them a hard sell. Pages that are filled with sales language like "Buy Now," "Why we are the best," "We are number one," versus "Educational tips, blogs or video," "Testimonials from your customers," "A story or video on what an experience is like for your customer," has far greater value. Provide useful content that lets them know they're in the right place. Position yourself as an expert in your field with quality, well-written articles, content and video. Keep your pages as free of distractions as possible. *What do you want your website to do once I'm on it*? Your call to action should be the most important element of the page.

3. Images and Clip Art

When using images and clip art on your site, make sure you use only royalty-free artwork or work you own the rights to. Be wary of sites that offer free stock photos. Many of them allow uploading of stolen images that the "author" has no rights to. Always make sure you get permission from the true owner of an image before using it anywhere on your site. Ask us for suggestions of clip art sites we use.

4. Videos

Video marketing is one of the hottest new trends in internet businesses. Video marketing grabs your visitor and offers a more direct message than words. A professionally made video adds an extra layer of professionalism and credibility to your product or service. Videos that use whiteboard animation are especially effective in engaging their audience. Best of all – *you do not have to be in the video to have a video*! Whether you are promoting a product or service, offering customer testimonials, or just want to show your passion for your topic of choice, videos engage and entertain your visitors. Here is an example of a "whiteboard video" - http://youtu.be/9XH_imD3UVI

5. Use Social Media

Today, shareable content is what visitors seek. Make it easy for your visitors to share your posts and articles with others by including social media sharing buttons on your website. This will draw even more visitors to your site from sites like Pinterest, Twitter, Facebook, and more. Social networking is also an excellent way to market your business. Remember when using social media, the intent is to engage and entertain, not sell. People who like your social media profiles will click through to your website out of sheer curiosity. And if your site provides something of value, they'll check it out further and become a loyal brand follower!

6. Online Web Presence

Help improve your website's ranking in Google and other search engines by formatting your content properly. Long blocks of complex information can drive your visitors away. Break up your content by adding sub-headers, numbered lists, and bullet points. This will make the content easier to scan by readers and search engines alike, and improve your ranking. Of course, this all begins with selecting a well-researched keyword. Use keyword tools to select keywords for your site that don't have too much competition, but enough people searching for the term to make your website visible. Make sure you have someone on your team that understands the fundamentals of what drives your site to the top pages of search engines.

7. Encourage Your Visitors to Come Back

The best way to encourage visitors to come back is to offer them something. An e-newsletter, contests, freebies, logo merchandise, the list of ideas is endless, and only bound by your creativity. I love using Constant Contact to build my e-mail distribution list as well as stay in touch with my followers.

Online marketing isn't comprised of just one task, but many put together. By following the above tips, you should start to see more visitors to your site and an improvement in search engine rankings.

CHAPTER 5:
Website vs Social Media

It used to be that having a website alone was enough.

But will your new customers find you today if they Google keywords relevant to your business?

Think about it. If I wanted to find the best ***mom recommended author*** and I put those words into Google or YouTube, what comes up?

Now if you want to do your own homework or see how popular a certain business is what do you do?

- Do you look at Google keyword results or images?
- Do you look at how many social media links this person or business has listed alongside their name?
- What makes you decide to do business with a stranger on the Internet such as a legal service, where you will go for travel, or who you will choose to be your real estate agent?

Your customers can sell your business better than you can. That is one of the benefits of social media and building a strong web-based presence. Consumers generally trust and rely on ***Yelp*** (another color in the box of social media colors) and other review sites before they trust or do business with you.

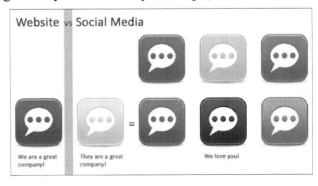

Now I am not discounting word of mouth and honest referrals at all. These are significant and every business relies on repeat business. Some businesses may not need the colors of social media because they have so much business they would not want more. If that is not you, and you do want more business, could handle more

Website vs Social Media

business if you grew, or would want to be more profitable if you could, then this is the right chapter for you.

92% of Americans have some type of online presence by the age of two. ***More than a third of them had a digital life before they were born.*** (Source: http://mashable.com/2010/10/07/toddlers-online-presence)

Take a look at an introduction for apps for a child as young as 3. Here is a link to the ***top ten apps of 2013 for kids (ages 3 to 12)***: (Source: http://www.usatoday.com/story/tech/columnist/gudmundsen/2013/12/25/kid-apps-best-of-2013/3957451)

These children are going to grow up one day. How are they going to find your business, 10, 15, 20 years from now? I know that is a long time to plan ahead, but this can show you how many 20 and 30-year-olds will be using technology to quickly find what they want?

Statistics On Digital Media Usage

More and more Americans get their news online these days. Fifty percent of the public now cites the Internet as a main source for national and international news, still below television, but far above newspapers and radio.

71% of those 18-29 cite the Internet as a main news source, more than the percentage that cites television (55%). Among those 30-49, 63% say the Internet is where they go to get most of their news, matching for the first time, the percentage who say television is their top news source. Older Americans have been slower to embrace the internet as a main news source.

More American adults consume news on mobile: 64% of tablet owners and 62% of smartphone owners said they got news on their devices in 2012. 73% of tablet owners read in-depth articles at least sometimes, including 19% who did so daily. 61% of smartphone news consumers at least sometimes read longer stories, 11% regularly.

Social media has grown as a source for news: 19% of Americans saw news on a ***social network*** "yesterday" in 2012, more than double the

9% who had done so in 2010. Those in their 30s (30%) are nearly as likely as those 18-24 (34%) to say they saw news or news headlines on Facebook or another social networking site yesterday.
(Source: http://www.pewresearch.org/fact-tank/2013/10/16/12-trends-shaping-digital-news)

74% of consumers rely on some type of social media, according to Pew Research. Consumers rely on social media and their mobile devices via the web to research and evaluate products and services before even visiting your web site.

Businesses can no longer operate under the assumption that content on their site, along with carefully crafted marketing messages, are the most influential and trusted sources of information for today's smart consumer. Those that do may be leaving customers and revenue behind.

Your Website

Most small-business owners have neither the time nor the technical skills to learn code and build a proper website from the ground up. One of the first places to look at is your website. How updated or modern is it? Just because you have a website on the world wide web does not mean that you are instantly going to make money. How is your customer going to find you? How are you going to drive traffic to your site?

While *social media* is the most common buzz phrase used today when discussing digital marketing, having an effective website is so important!

Webmaster Aaron Doucette writes:

Website vs Social Media

Social media is obviously important and can have a significant and immediate impact. I equate selling on social media to trying to sell to someone from a kiosk in a shopping mall - the person is already preoccupied and there are endless distractions vying for their attention.

When you can get the potential customer to your website, it is like you are sitting with them at their kitchen table. You have gained their full attention and can effectively communicate your call-to-action, you can fully communicate your brand. Your social media channels should therefore be a vehicle to get people to your own website as often as possible.

Recognizing that the true value of your website content lies primarily in its SEO strength might come as a revelation to many website owners. Thinking about a sales-oriented site -- isn't the primary function of any content performed *before* the visitor arrives on your site – you want your business to show up as a result in a search engine? Half of the sale is made right there on Google. Once on your site, it is easy to lead a visitor through the sales process with appropriate call-to-action messages.

Why is the call-to-action so important to designing your site? Every website owner wants to 'sell' you something. Even an amateur blog wants you to become their 'customer' by subscribing and returning for fresh content. For the business owner, the primary function of a website is to convert visitors to leads, and ultimately to sales. Often a business owner will fill a website with valuable information and get traffic to their site, but not see any sales as a result. The reason? They have no effective call-to-action. If you aren't asking your visitors to call you, email you, or click the 'buy now' button it is unlikely that they are going to do so.

Many people do not realize how affordable a website today can be! In the mid 2000's you could have paid $5,000 for a cheap website. Today you can build a website for $500 to $5,000 depending upon your business needs. If you need a shopping cart or e-commerce component built in, then you would not be in this pricing category. There are also many YouTube do it yourself tutorials for creating your own websites. You can also use template sites such as SquareSpace, Homestead, and WordPress.

For example, WordPress is a free and popular content-management system that can significantly cut the amount of time it takes to get your site going. Designers have created a host of templates (known in WordPress as *themes*) that you may use to create or spruce up a website – many are free or low cost.

Ask to see work samples and get recommendations before you hire anyone and be upfront about your budget. Offer to let the designer use your site as a portfolio sample in exchange for a reduced rate.

Creating content is the most important feature for your website. A website used to be like your business card. Today it is an informational holding place that will not get noticed if you do not do many of the 360 elements I talk about throughout this book.

The design and content of your site is more important than just having a site.

When you hire someone to create your website, they should know about your business, who you are, and what your goals are when one visits your site. If they do not seem interested in learning about your business, they are probably the wrong people to design your website.

And never let them own or rent back your URL. You must own it yourself to protect your brand.

Website vs Social Media
Improve How Your Site Looks On Mobile Devices

Many websites can be a bit hard to view on a mobile device like the iPhone. By improving the layout of your site and optimizing it for mobile, you will be able to ensure that you get better responses when people visit your site on a mobile device. Mobile devices are accounting for a larger percentage of web usage every day.

"Our only limitations are those we set up in our own minds."
~Napoleon Hill

CHAPTER 6:
Full Circle

It takes many of these circles – these colors – to make your business. Some are right for you and others are not. The 360 graph shows the pieces your business should address, whether you are a startup or an established business.

A good set of questions that you can use on your own are the **established business owner questions** on the next few pages. Tailor this to your own business team, associates, and so forth. These are some of the common questions I use when interviewing almost any business.

Go back to the basics of your business. What makes your business stand out from the rest? What kind of messages define who you are? What is your purpose? What is your business's motto?

You can do the same by asking your employees questions. Ask your associates to get involved in planning your mission statement.

At the end of the day, you can have all the technology in place, but if your customer does not connect with your business or your employees they may overlook you and go with a competitor who takes the time to have a humanistic approach and uses digital and social tools within their business.

When *LIFE* was founded in 1883, it was a general-interest magazine, heavy on illustrations, jokes, and social commentary. It featured some of the greatest writers, editors, and cartoonists of its era.

Here is one of my favorite mottos. It talks about its purpose for the company, employees, and its readers. The motto of the first issue of *LIFE* was: "While there's Life, there's hope." The new magazine set forth its principles and policies to its readers.

> *We wish to have some fun in this paper... We shall try to domesticate as much as possible of the casual cheerfulness that is drifting about in an unfriendly*

Full Circle

world... We shall have something to say about religion, about politics, fashion, society, literature, the stage, the stock exchange, and the police station, and we will speak out what is in our mind as fairly, as truthfully, and as decently as we know how.

(Source: Wikipedia)

As a company, ask yourself what defines you or your business. And then ask, does it speak to a customer base?

A common element I find with many businesses who have been in business a long time is that business owners get stale. They get worn out. And it can trickle down to their employees.

"Individual commitment to a group effort – that is what makes a team work." – Vince Lombardi

"The biggest mistake made in marketing – and a reason that success can be so elusive – is ***to not clearly explain who you are and what you offer***."

This is what Maribeth Kuzmeski's says in her article, *What is Your Simple, Repeatable Statement of Value*?

> What is your elevator speech? When you are at a networking event or when someone asks you, "What do you do?" What is your answer?

A colleague of mine, Scot Shier, a financial planner, often says "The best way to have someone walk away from me is to start off a conversation with "Hi, I'm a financial planner. I recognize that I have to have a better pitch and constantly strive to make it better."

> Kuzmeski validates this point saying, "When that question is asked, your black and white answer actually causes people to want to talk with you *less*!" Therefore, "*If you know that your answer will have a negative response, why don't you say something different?*"

Your business needs to have a refined story to assist in marketing your story and obtaining clients. But, there is a serious need to have a compelling opening line for your story - probably several of them.

> "Without something compelling (to them), you may never get the chance to share your story."

> Kuzmeski's gives the following 4-step formula for building your own *Simple, Repeatable, Statement of Value* (SRSV). It is a solution for compelling others to want to listen to you. Develop your 15-20 second (SRSV) for each target audience.

An SRSV is a statement that is easy to remember and shares some value directly for the person you are speaking with. Your SRSV may not include the answer to every question, and it does not have to be compiled in this order.

Full Circle

SRSV Builder Questions:
1. Who are you?
2. What do you do?
3. Who do you work with?
4. What is interesting about what you do?

Let's turn the Financial Advisor's Answer Into: *"I work with family-owned businesses, helping them pay less in taxes and protect their assets. I specifically work with those with serious profit problems... Big profits."*

Example 2: *"I am a financial advisor and our firm works with families to help them mitigate risk and protect their legacy. We work with some of the wealthiest families in California - in money and values. Our business is built solely on referrals and from the communities we serve.*

Example 3: *"I am a financial advisor with Quintessential Financial. The name Quintessential comes from the fact that I have quintuplets. My firm specializes in working with corporate executives who want to have freedom when they retire."*

Example 4: *"I am an adjunct professor, head the chamber of commerce for my city, and also help people as their financial advisor. I get to teach people how to plan for their retirement. Having put 5 children through college recently, we help parents structure their college planning as well."*

- All four of these are actual SRSV's that give quick and reasonably clear initial descriptions of what they do.
- All share with the listener who they specialize in working with - a powerful tool in framing your unique position.
- All end with something hopefully interesting to the person they are speaking with.

By focusing on a short, memorable, and compelling description of your company, you will find that it is easier to open the door to a stream of referrals, new clients, and sales. Taking the time to focus on your company story and your *Simple, Repeatable, Statement of Value* messaging can bring a return on investment far superior to that of many other activities you do in your business!

> *"Business is the most creative and challenging pursuit in which one can engage. It is also downright fun (if done right)! – Michael Gerber, The E-Myth Enterprise*

If you tell me, "I'm in business to make lots of money," you are foolish or you need to reestablish your mission and purpose. Money is the reward that comes from your work.

Here are some questions that should help you redefine your business.

These answers can help any marketing entity learn your brand – your messages – and help develop appropriate content. Authenticity is appreciated.

Established Business Owner Questions

This information helps establish *who you are* for website development, message planning, branding, and so forth. Often times, it helps you simply get back to the basics of where you have been and where you want your brand to go.

1. Describe your background and education.

2. What are the strengths of the members on your team?

3. What would your clients say they like about working with you?

4. What is your mission or purpose for being in your business? Why do you do what you do?

5. What message would you like your customers to receive from your business?

6. Have you created the same message across all your social outlets and website? (Are your Twitter, Instagram, and other social media sites using the same consistent name, logo and brand?)

Full Circle

7. What is presently good about your business?

8. What could be going better with your business?

9. How long do you plan to stay in this business?

10. What happens to the business when you are done with it?

11. How do you acquire new customers? Explain the process of your customer acquisition.

12. What are your greatest business strengths – those that cause your customers to want to do business with you? What are your main skill set and *gifts*?

13. What are the main weaknesses in your business – the ones that limit your sales, growth, or profitability? (If I were interviewing you, what might you humbly reveal that you do *not* know about your business?)

14. What are your areas of greatest opportunity for the future, based on the trends in your business? What do you want to be known for?

15. What are the three biggest worries or concerns you have about your business today?

16. What is your specific competitive advantage? What should it be? What could it be?

17. What sets the speed at which you achieve your top three business goals?

18. Give at least one story and results about how you helped someone in the community (it could be something outside the scope of your business):

19. Do you have mentors that helped shape your business foundation? Please discuss.

20. Who is YOUR ideal client?

21. Who is your competition?

22. What sets you apart from your competition?

23. What business KEYWORDS would someone use to find you on the Internet or on Google, for example?

Business Startup Questions

This set of questions can help any marketer or team learn about your business. Answer the questions authentically. This information helps identify *who you are* for planning, messages, and business development.

1. What are the strengths of the members on your team?

2. What is your mission or purpose for your business?

3. Who is YOUR ideal customer?

4. What are your greatest business strengths – those that will cause your customers to want to do business with you? What are your main skill set and *gifts*?

5. What are the main weaknesses in your business – the ones that would limit your sales, growth or profitability?

6. What are your areas of greatest opportunity for the future, based on the trends in your business? What do you want to be known for?

7. What are the three biggest worries or concerns one would have about your business today?

8. What is your specific competitive advantage? What should it be? What could it be?

9. What would you need to make your top 3 business goals happen?

10. Give a story on how you foresee your business idea helping someone.

11. Do you have mentors that helped shape your business foundation? Who are they? What would you want the world to know about them?

12. Please share or add anything pertinent that would help you grow your network of people in business today and in the near future.

Full Circle

13. What is relevant in helping your business direction's goals and ideas?

> ***Training Tip:*** Think of your business as a journey that started with goals. You want to get from A to Z in a certain amount of time. Jotting down your goals is so imperative! It can help keep you accountable for the steps you need to attain. It can overwhelm you. Just like you would not go out and run a marathon tomorrow without proper training, you cannot go from A to Z without proper planning. Start with steps A, B, and C, then the next chunks being D, E, F, G, and so forth. Eventually Z will come. And then your professional career takes off in ways unimagined. Z is the big pay off!

A goal is a dream with a deadline.

The following is a chart of where you might like marketing help. Mark an "X" next to the areas that interest you in growing your business.

Social Media	Media Interview
▪ *i.e.* Instagram, Twitter messages, LinkedIn®, Facebook Pages, Pinterest, etc.	▪ Video or audio based interview so the public can see who you are behind your brand.
Blog	**Website improvement**
▪ Posts, articles, write ups, community stories, incorporating your own network, vendors, etc.	▪ Content ▪ Video based ▪ Branding
Content Development & Branding	**Speaking**
▪ Helping you write your website ▪ Helping you create or develop proper and ongoing relevant messages to your contacts and new prospects ▪ Developing a relevant brand ▪ Logo	▪ Speaking presentations to business groups that could benefit from your services. ▪ Helping you develop materials for presentations or speaking opportunities.
Helping Others	**Community**
▪ Developing tools to connect you to a bigger network. ▪ Gaining referrals from your existing clientele. ▪ Teaching others *(how what you do can help them generate more time, business, rewards, profits).*	▪ Helping other organization(s) as you grow. ▪ Networking with like-minded individuals. ▪ Being on local boards who will in turn help your business's brand gain community awareness and exposure. ▪ Conferences and/or trade shows.
Accountability	**Referrals**
▪ Creating steps to keep you focused on the parts of the business that need you most so you can effectively grow.	▪ Being introduced to new prospects and your ideal clientele.

Wherever you marked an *X*, each of those items will be driven by Content Marketing. (*see CHAPTER 12: Content Is The New Black*)

Full Circle

Which ones give you more business?

When using the "color" of social media – you may not have time to log in and out of each Platform to stay consistent.

You may want to outsource this so you can focus on your business. Often times I find businesses worry about their Facebook or Twitter and will spend hours on end in this area, versus spending time developing their business.

4 Ways To Make The Most Out Of Social Media

Social media sites are great for businesses or even individuals, but in order to make the most of them and not get lost in them, there are a few important things that should be taken into consideration:

1. Have a Focus

What is the point of having numerous of social media profiles if you do not use them properly to engage with your customers? It is important that you have a focus on the tasks you want to take on.

2. Schedule Out Your Posts and Messages

Yes, take advantage of all the features social media channels provide to their users, especially when it comes to posts. There are a couple of websites that can help you schedule and monitor your posts across all your social media streams. There are two sites causing a lot of buzz among consumers for effectiveness: HootSuite and TweetDeck are "dashboard" websites that allow you to send out multiple messages at the click of a button.

They are free or have upgraded features. You can schedule and send out a message days or months in advance and choose which "social media streams" to use. It is a really great way to not have to be "on" all the time.

3. Get Help

If you opt to do every task by yourself no matter how small it is, it will take a lot of your valuable time, which will prevent you from doing other things. For this matter, try to obtain outside help. The more helping hands you can get in your team, the better it will be for your business and you. If you lack a big team, try outsourcing the tedious or the big tasks so that you can move on to the next important thing on your list.

4. Think Ahead Regarding Content

Once your business begins to become more and more successful, having draft posts saved can be of great help when something goes wrong in the office.

Reputation Management

Look great when employers, customers, and prospects Google you.

Yelp and Google Reviews are the most popular online sites that will generate and post to the world positive or negative reviews about your product or service.

Be sure that your business is registered with Google and is listed on Google Maps.

Yelp Tip: Make sure you fill out your *free* Yelp business profile so that you get found online. People ask me about Yelp all the time. "Do I need to subscribe to it?" The short answer is, it depends on your business industry. If you do not have good customer service or do not look at the online identity that others are creating for you via Yelp, you may be in trouble. Regardless, your business should always pay attention and respond positively to what others are saying about you. Someone at your company needs to be responsible for responding to good and bad reviews. Often times I find that no one wants to take on this job, the company does nothing and the reviews spiral downward.

Full Circle

What Google Knows About You

Google knows a lot about you. And if you use any Google properties or have in the past, you may want to know some of what they track and where they track it.

Go to www.Google.com/Dashboard and log in with your Google credentials (Gmail, YouTube, Blogger, or whatever you use to access any Google properties; probably your Gmail address). This is your Google dashboard and shows many of the things Google knows about you.

It knows your websites, your Google Analytics profile, your Gmail contacts, and any Google properties that you have claimed, such as YouTube. You can access your saved Google Alerts, see your Android phone information, and even check out your Google Voice number.

If you are a regular Google product user, it is an interesting look to see how tied in you are to all their search products.

LinkedIn®

It is a really great business social networking site to stay connected with business people. Make sure your profile is up to date and looks professional. I have personally spent over one hundred hours creating and updating my profile, and I have received plenty of business leads from my profile. Remember, you get one chance to make a first impression. In business, it has to be done professionally and visually.

There are two sentences that are great to use when you connect with someone on LinkedIn who you want to meet:
- *How may I support you?*
- *Who is your ideal client?*

It is so easy to ask someone about *them* as a conversation and meeting starter.

The goal is to connect with your customers, fans and prospects – so you stand out!

Valuable LinkedIn® Tips Because 1st Impressions Count

Do not underestimate the power of LinkedIn® for building your business network to engage and meet people you would otherwise have not met. LinkedIn® is a valuable resource for small businesses.

I have spent countless hours on my LinkedIn® profile, not for vanity reasons, but rather to make a lasting first impression. I have received business from my LinkedIn® profile, creating value for the hard work my team has put into it, as a source for *branding* who I am, who my company is, who I hope to meet, and how I can help others in my fields of interest. Besides that, when one searches your name on Google, did you know that your LinkedIn® profile (if you have created one) will most likely pop up on page 1 of Google? This can happen for you as well.

Content is becoming increasingly important to LinkedIn®. The introduction of 'Influencer posts' where Leaders such as Richard Branson share their wisdom and thought leadership is evidence of LinkedIn's desire to make the site increasingly content rich, rather than the slightly dull platform it has been perceived as in previous years.

There are 60 million users using LinkedIn! 30 million alone in the U.S.! These are professionals with an average household income of $107,000. (Source: http://www.pewinternet.org/fact-sheets/social-networking-fact-sheet)

When you think of social media, you hear people say, "I don't want to be sold, I want to have a conversation, engage, and interact with people that can help me, make me laugh, help me grow, and who care about me and what I do."

More Linkedin Tips

1. Make sure your LinkedIn® has a professional photograph. Spend the time, energy, and dollars to make this stand out. The photo

should not be one where other people are cropped out. Remember, when one searches your name on Google, your LinkedIn® is usually the top network that will pop out to someone.

2. Think of LinkedIn as your snapshot of your recent and past success. It is beyond a resume.

3. Take advantage of adding links, videos, and more!

4. Make connections. Once you are logged into your e-mail account, LinkedIn® will suggest connections in *add connections*.

5. Update your profile with *required details* as much as possible.

6. *Join groups* that are related to your business or niche. Utilizing advanced search options for adding users from same niche or business can help in having targeted users on your list. Do not add countless members at a time. You may violate terms and conditions of LinkedIn® by doing so.

7. *When you meet someone* and take their business card, I like to *connect* with them via LinkedIn® within a few days and also write them via e-mail. LinkedIn® shows your website and your social media links. Make sure they are all updated and relevant to your brand. If something is personal and not part of your brand, make the decision to remove it or place it elsewhere at the bottom of your LinkedIn® page.

8. To create *brand awareness* you should be active in 3-5 LinkedIn® groups consistently – share good content, discussions, and other interactions – be a contributor and thought leader.

9. *Ask at least three people*, your employees or colleagues to look at your LinkedIn® profile. Ask them for feedback and suggestions. Be open to their changes and let them contribute their ideas.

10. *Build a presence* for your business on LinkedIn®. Endorse people you know and recommend people (see graphic below).

11. Take the time to say, *"Thank You."* If you hired someone and they are on LinkedIn, offer to write a testimonial as a professional courtesy. This goes a long way!

12. *Create your page*, attract followers, and post company updates to drive engagement.

13. ***Company Pages*** offer public information about each company on LinkedIn. You should clearly state the objectives and focus of the organization. If you manage different entities, you want to have a company page, this is separate from your personal LinkedIn® profile, yet it is connected by you. Filling your personal and LinkedIn® company page with compelling and interesting status updates about your ***industry or business*** requires ongoing management, but it is the most effective way to grow followers for your page and increase your company's visibility. As you

---

Add a Company

Company Pages offer public information about each company on LinkedIn. To add a Company Page, please enter the company name and your email address at this company. Only current employees are eligible to create a Company Page.

Company name:

[   ]

Your email address at company:

[   ]

☐ I verify that I am the official representative of this company and have the right to act on behalf of my company in the creation of this page.

---

grow your following, remember to segment your members and target them with more relevant updates.

14. ***Set up a Showcase Page to Better Segment Your Product or Service.*** A showcase page is a unique destination on LinkedIn focused on a specific audience. Showcase pages have a two-column layout to highlight more content shared, instead of allowing for any functionality for careers, products or services. To start a showcase page, visit your company page as an admin, and from the "Edit" pull-down menu at the top right, select "Create a Showcase Page." From here, upload a unique hero image and description to help brand your showcase pages uniquely from the main company page of your business. Currently your business can create up to 10 showcase pages for your organization and receive analytics for each business. The page is connected to your main company page with a link at the top of the page.

15. ***Sponsor Updates from LinkedIn® Showcase Pages.*** Begin planning how often your company will sponsor updates on your

Full Circle

showcase pages as a part of your overall LinkedIn® ad budget to help grow your audience. Before deciding to start a showcase page for the audiences that make up your customer base, ask yourself a few honest questions to determine if it is the right move for your organization. Your business will ideally need enough talent and resources to manage a showcase page and to decide if it's necessary. Your audience should be thoroughly developed on LinkedIn® in order for it to be worth your time.

16. ***Invite existing employees, clients or customers, vendors and partners to follow your page***, and showcase it to relevant LinkedIn® members. If it's appropriate and/or allowable, ask key clients, colleagues or customers to recommend your products and services on your LinkedIn® company page. These recommendations show up on your page for everyone to see. This can serve as powerful testimonials for your business.

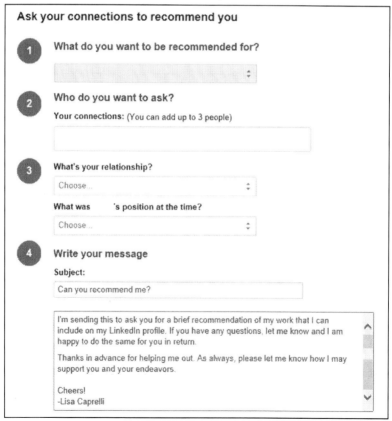

17. ***Recommend*** people you know and ask them to write a recommendation for you. I am surprised at how many people overlook this *free* feature! This is different than the ***endorse*** feature on LinkedIn. Once you are logged into your LinkedIn account, go to ***profile***, then click on ***edit profile*** and ***ask to be recommended***.

If you want to recommend someone, you type in their name at the top of LinkedIn[®]:

You click on ***send a message***. Then you scroll to ***recommend*** and LinkedIn easily helps you choose features.

As with any social media platform *make a decision to focus on one or two aspects of LinkedIn, such as networking and engaging in discussions in 3-5 LinkedIn[®] groups maximum.*

With limited resources, it will become extremely time consuming to attempt to work in more than 3 groups, whilst searching for new prospects – using Advanced search, checking who has viewed your profile, and posting status updates.

Also, decide which aspects of LinkedIn will help you to engage with the right business connections and focus on these only.

Full Circle

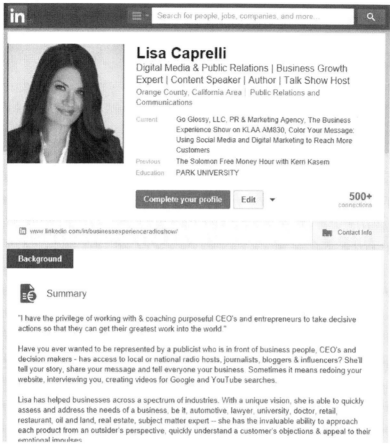

Summary

"I have the privilege of working with & coaching purposeful CEO's and entrepreneurs to take decisive actions so that they can get their greatest work into the world."

Have you ever wanted to be represented by a publicist who is in front of business people, CEO's and decision makers - has access to local or national radio hosts, journalists, bloggers & influencers? She'll tell your story, share your message and tell everyone your business. Sometimes it means redoing your website, interviewing you, creating videos for Google and YouTube searches.

Lisa has helped businesses across a spectrum of industries. With a unique vision, she is able to quickly assess and address the needs of a business, be it, automotive, lawyer, university, doctor, retail, restaurant, oil and land, real estate, subject matter expert -- she has the invaluable ability to approach each product from an outsider's perspective, quickly understand a customer's objections & appeal to their emotional impulses

Snapshots of Lisa's LinkedIn Profile

CHAPTER 7:
Black & White vs Color

Today you have all these colors available to use in your business. A huge palette of colors exist at your fingertips for your business – not just black and white. For example: blue for Facebook, teal for Twitter, navy for LinkedIn, and red for YouTube. Then let us add colors for Pinterest, Instagram, WordPress, Blogger, Google, and Google Plus.

Think of every color as a tool. Could your business survive with just black and white? What would the world be like if it was only black and white? What happens when you add a little bit of color into to your life?

With that said, I want you to have an open mind about what you don't know. You don't know what you don't know. Oftentimes, people fear what they don't know or understand.

Business owners who have not opened up to these ideas tell me:
- *Social media is ineffective.*
- *It's just a fad.*
- *Social media doesn't work.*
- *I had someone do it for me and it didn't help.*
- *I don't need to do it.*
- *I don't understand it.*
- *My friends or clients don't use it.*

That is exactly my point! You are missing out on a whole group or groups of people not *finding you*!

Social media and inbound marketing techniques have been great tools for marketers. Not only do leads generated through social and content

Black & White vs Color

marketing typically cost less than half as much as traditional outbound-generated leads, they can also close at a higher rate. Social media is not just about lead generation. While your prospective customer is using search keywords and social media to research products and services before making purchase decisions, marketers and public relations professionals can use those same tools to research buyer wants and needs.

If you are an *experienced business* owner and not using these tools, ask yourself:

- *Do you plan on retiring anytime soon?*
- *Do you plan on being in business 5, 10, or 15 years from now?*
- *Do you plan to pass your business on to someone? What colors will you have included to make it easier for them to take over?*
- *What have you really branded if you are not using the colors?*
- *Will your business actually be unnoticeable and worth less?*
- *What kind of systems and tools are you leaving in place for the next person who takes it over?*
- *Do you think if you used some of these* **colors** *it would bring more value to your credibility, who you are and so forth?*

Now, if you still do not think this is important, I promise you, your 24-year-old competitor just out of college thinks it is important and will act on it!

Who are we going to find, if it is not you, when we are searching for keywords on the Internet? Here are a sample string of words, *keywords* one might type or speak into the search field of a search engine:

- *Wills and trust attorney in Newport Beach*
- *Happy hour in Old Town Orange*
- *Mom recommended author*
- *Estate planning tips in Los Angeles*
- *Oil change in Whittier*
- *Party planning ideas*
- *Radio show host Orange County*
- *Should I lease or buy a car?*

We should find YOU versus your competition. Especially if you have more experience over a 20-something-year-old. Not that I am discounting a young business owner; I love entrepreneurship of all ages. However, the 20, 30, 40 year experienced business person may not understand how to get found online as easily as the young entrepreneur. There are more than a few teenage entrepreneurs that got rich by getting found. Google it.

Credibility

Let's face it, the phrase *Google It* is part of our everyday lives. Maybe you want someone to introduce you to a business referral, or your colleague says, you have got to meet this person! What is the first thing many of us do – whether we use our mobile device or the computer?

We Google your name and business, or we Google keywords on the search fields. If nothing pops up on Google or YouTube, I say to myself, "Well if this person or business was truly as professional as they claim, why haven't they taken the time to invest in their name – their brand?

We live in a society where first impressions count. It takes only a minute to make an impression and much longer to change it. Think of your business as a person you are just meeting. Before you even speak, you made a judgment based on appearances, and it is in the first minute that you may make up your mind about them.

Impressions count! They matter and can make a difference before someone decides if they want to work with you. The Internet has changed everything. Today it is about getting found with the right message you want to portray. It can be a strong competitive advantage.

These are some of the qualifiers your potential customer considers:
- *You are relevant if you are easily found online.*
- *You look like someone I want to work with.*
- *When I search your name after I find you, I see what images you share and who you are. This will tell me if I can trust you.*
- *You stand out from your competition.*

- *I may quickly learn things about you that make me want to do business with you.*

Type your name into a search engine on a computer. Now use your smart phone and repeat the search. What comes up? *Take the time to be in control of your brand* and what comes up in a search.

10,000 Hours

So you are an expert, now what?

The Beatles made themselves experts in their field by doing the same thing over and over again (their music) for 10,000+ hours. So if 10,000 hours makes you an expert that is roughly 4.8 years at 40 hours a week. If you worked 20 hours a week 10,000 hours would take you less than 10 years. However, what entrepreneur works less than 20 hours a week?

At a 40 hour a week work week, to keep it simple, let's do some math on your subject matter level of experience, in the form of lifetime hours:

- *1 year's experience, that translates into 2080 hours*
- *10 years' experience, that translates into 20,800 hours*
- *20 years' experience, that translates into 41,600 hours*
- *30 years' experience, that translates into 62,400 hours*
- *40 years' experience, that translates into 83,200 hours*

More debate: So are you telling me that with this many hours of experience behind you that you are going to let the 24-year-old or the 34-year-old out of college make more money than you because we are able to find them on the Internet and use their services?

Please help me find you! If I am having surgery or I want an expert party planner or I need a financial professional, I want to find the right person and so do millions of other people. However, if we cannot find you, we will find your competition who invested the time to use the tools throughout this book to get found because they either understand the tools, or they outsourced someone to use the tools for them.

CHAPTER 8:
Statistics & Data

Here are some statistics and data for you to ponder in your business:

We live in a world of generational equity. There is a generational gap.

Think of how this data could and would apply to your business if you took the time to understand them.

- What target age is your customer base?
- Who do you want it to be?
- Could your business be marketed to other age groups or cultures if you changed your message to one that they understand?
- What influence does each generational divide have when deciding where to spend its dollar?

Numbers tell stories. The young and old do not think, look or vote alike…or choose the same products or services to buy. It is important to look at the data that affects every one of us at every phase of our lives. We are a country of immigrants, 40 million people since the 1965 immigration wave, which was the biggest in history.

Hispanics are the largest and youngest minority group in the United States. One-in-five school children is Hispanic. One-in-four newborns is Hispanic. Never before in this country's history has a minority ethnic group made up so large a share of the youngest Americans. By force of numbers alone, the kinds of adults these young Latinos become will help shape the kind of society America becomes in the 21st century.
Young Latinos are satisfied with their lives, optimistic about their futures and place a high value on

Statistics & Data

education, hard work, and career success. Yet they are much more likely than other American youths to drop out of school and to become teenage parents. They are more likely than white and Asian youths to live in poverty.

(Source: http://www.pewhispanic.org/2009/12/11/between-two-worlds-how-young-latinos-come-of-age-in-america)

The nation's population will rise to 438 million in 2050, from 296 million in 2005, and fully 82% of the growth during this period will be due to immigrants arriving from 2005 to 2050 and their descendants. Of the 117 million people added to the population during this period due to the effect of new immigration, 67 million will be the immigrants themselves, 47 million will be their children and 3 million will be their grandchildren.

Interracial marriages are becoming more common. One quarter of Hispanics marry outside their own culture as compared to Asians at 28 percent.

Essentially, just as I am, we are a nation of mixed diversity. I call myself a mutt and laugh. Diversity has its strength.

By 2060 it is predicted that half a million people will be over the age 100. There will be as many people over the age of 85 as much as there are under the age of five.

Life expectancy in 1900 was that you would live to be 49 years of age. In 2009 that number was 79 years of age.

Generations tend to be about 20 years in length and are shaped by the historical events people experience at roughly the same stage in their life cycle.

Here is the median net worth of households headed by these types of generations:

If You Were Born	Your Generation Is	Median Net Worth
Before 1946	The Silents	$173,000
From 1946 to 1964	Baby Boomers	$118,000
1960s to early 1980s	Generation X	$30,000
Born after 1989 – The youngest and biggest group since the Baby Boomers	Millennials	$4,000

(Source: Paul Taylor: The Next Generation)

Think of this: 10,000 baby boomers turn 65 every day, today, tomorrow until the year 2030. What does this mean for your life, business and opportunities?

Millennials & The Differences Among Other Age Groups

Saturday morning cartoons are replaced with an iPad or smart phone.

Millennials are digital natives!

Grew up with cell phones and more technology than any of the previous generations.

Born into social networking era.

They are highly educated because of the economic struggles of their times.

Less religiously affiliated than any other generational group.

Only 25% are married. Compare this data to grandparents whose statistics said 50% were married by a young age. Why do they not marry young? When polled, the overwhelming response is the country's *economic foundation.*
Many go home after college to live with mom and dad due to lack of jobs.

Interview With Teen "Bailey"

Let us take a look at an interview with 17-year-old, Bailey Paxton. Bailey is a motivated leader who is interested in owning his own business one day. Bailey followed an entrepreneur around for 10 days and he attended a Teen Entrepreneur Academy business camp at Concordia University in Irvine. Here is a perspective from a future businessman.

What do you see as the value of being an entrepreneur versus working for someone else? There is so much value in being an entrepreneur versus working for someone else. Personally, I believe that in life if you don't build your own dreams, someone else will hire you to help them build theirs. Entrepreneurship allows you to take **your** dreams and make them a reality.

What are the biggest skills in which you feel a business owner should invest? Obviously there are many important skills in which a business owner should invest. Examples of these include: hard work, perseverance, communication skills, listening, and having the right team. These are all important skills, however, I believe that the most important skill that a business owner should invest in is being a kind and sincere person. This is because when you meet someone, you never know when you will run into them down the road and how they can help you.

What do you think the seasoned professional does not understand about social media as you see it today? From my Grandma (who owns a golf course) I've learned that often times, she doesn't understand what a huge impact social media has on their business and how it can help it grow.

What is the value of an App to you and your peers? Mobile apps make life easier. With the tap of your screen, you can have access to an unlimited wealth of information. There is a difference between an app and a website. Time spent on a mobile device by the average US consumer has risen to 2 hours and 42 minutes per day. Apps continued to cement their lead, and commanded 86% of the average US mobile consumer's time, or 2 hours and 19 minutes per day. Time spent on the mobile web continued to decline and averaged just 14% of the US mobile consumer's time, or 22 minutes per day. The data tells a clear story that apps, are completely dominating mobile, and the browser has become a single application swimming in a sea of apps. (Source: http://www.flurry.com/bid/109749/Apps-Solidify-Leadership-Six-Years-into-the-Mobile-Revolution#.U9cXjoBdUxo)

Why do you feel more and more Millennials are not opting in or dropping out of using Facebook? I think the answer is pretty obvious if you think about it. It's because the older generations started to use it. What teenager wants to be monitored by a parent or family member?

What do you feel that the experienced businessperson can teach you that you would not otherwise know? An experienced businessperson has been there before. Because of that, they know what you are going through and will be able to help guide you through starting your business.

I learned that Entrepreneurship is really what you make of it. I personally think that entrepreneurs are the game changers. They are the ones inventing, innovating, and changing the world. In helping the company as an intern, one day, I was told to do what I considered meaningless tasks -- that someone else should do. It was then that I realized the people who would have normally done all of these things, were delegating them to me, so they could do more important things. After that I was content because I knew that one day I would be delegating less important tasks to others so I could spend more time on the important things.

Do you think it's significant that the experienced entrepreneur understand modern tools (such as YouTube, social media) and why? Of course it is significant that the experienced entrepreneur understands modern tools. It is so important because these tools provide so many opportunities that were not available in the past. We live in a world that is constantly changing and improving and an entrepreneur needs to stay ahead of the game.

Our generation, because of the information that we have access to, will be the most educated generation in the history of the world.

As it becomes ever more mobile, social networking is rapidly leaving the desktop in its wake. Currently, 68 percent of Facebook users spend their time accessing the service via mobile devices. Among Twitter users, this number rises to an impressive 86 percent. Just 2 percent of Instagram users use desktops. At the other end of the scale, LinkedIn is still very desktop based with 74 percent of its users accessing the professional network through PCs.

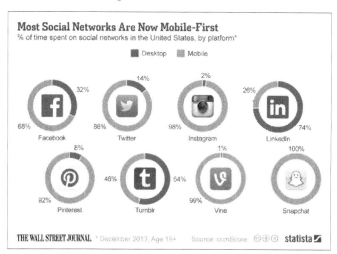

(Source: http://www.statista.com/chart/2109/time-spent-on-social-networks-by-platform/)

Understanding Changes

Who are your ideal customers? Is it important that you understand various ethnicities? Which cultures are you missing out on by not understanding this mix of colors in your business?

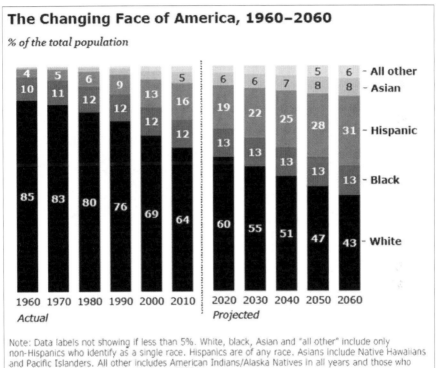

The Changing Face of America, 1960–2060

% of the total population

	1960	1970	1980	1990	2000	2010	2020	2030	2040	2050	2060
All other	4	5	6	9		5	6	6	7	5	6
Asian	10	11	12	12	13	16	19	22	25	8	8
Hispanic					12	12	13	13	13	28	31
Black	85	83	80	76	69	64	60	55	51	13	13
White										47	43

1960 1970 1980 1990 2000 2010 | 2020 2030 2040 2050 2060
Actual | *Projected*

Note: Data labels not showing if less than 5%. White, black, Asian and "all other" include only non-Hispanics who identify as a single race. Hispanics are of any race. Asians include Native Hawaiians and Pacific Islanders. All other includes American Indians/Alaska Natives in all years and those who reported two or more races beginning in 2000.

Source: Pew Research Center historic population estimates for 1960–1990 (Passel and Cohn, "US Population Projections: 2005-2050," Feb. 11, 2008). Census Bureau population estimates for 2000–2010 and projections for 2015-2060

Statistics & Data
America's Morphing Age Pyramid

Let us now look at an "age pyramid." Each bar represents a five year age cohort; with those ages 0-4 on the bottom and those ages 85 and older on the top. In every society since the start of history, whenever you broke down any population this way, you would always get a pyramid.

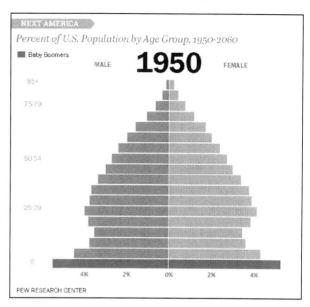

But from 1960 to 2060, our pyramid is changing into a rectangle. We will have almost as many Americans over age 85 as under age 5. This is the result of longer life spans and lower birthrates.

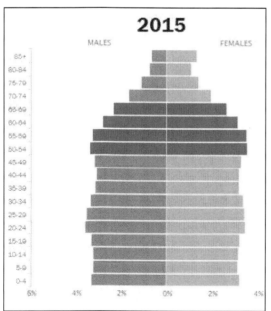

(Source: http://www.pewresearch.org/next-america/#Two-Dramas-in-Slow-Motion)

(See more related to the aging population in "The Next America.")

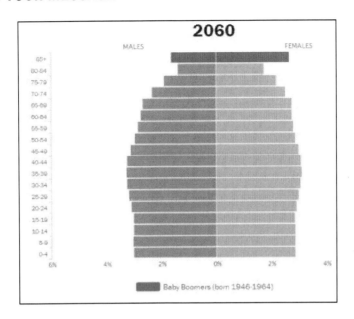

It used to be the generational divides were equivalent to a triangle. As you can see, according to the wonderful folks at Pew Research, that graph is changing year after year, decade after decade. For years it was a pyramid. Meaning at the top were very few people living to be to be 100.

As those demographics change into more of a rectangle of generational divides, it still goes to show you how the world has already changed.

- Is your business catering to as many cross sections as it can to get more business?
- There is "color" for everyone.
- Each row likes to be marketed to differently; Millennial customers differ from Baby Boomers, who differ from Generation X.

(Source: http://www.pewsocialtrends.org/2014/03/07/millennials-in-adulthood)

Statistics & Data

Millennials have...

Taken the lead in seizing new platforms of the digital era – the internet, mobile technology, social media – to construct personalized networks of friends, colleagues and groups.

They are "digital natives" – the only generation to have not had to adapt to these new technologies. Not surprisingly, they are the most avid users.

For example, 81% of Millennials are on Facebook, where their generation's median Facebook friend count is 250, far higher than that of older age groups.

Generations, Facebook and Friends

Median number of Facebook friends

Generation	Median
Millennial	250
Gen X	200
Younger Boomer	98
Older Boomer/Silent	50

Note: Based on Facebook users, n=960. In 2013, "Younger Boomers" were ages 49 to 57, "Older Boomers" were ages 58 to 67 and "Silents" were ages 68 to 85.

Source: Pew Research Center's Internet Project survey, Aug. 7-Sep. 16, 2013

PEW RESEARCH CENTER

Mobile Technology Fact Sheet

Here are some highlights from the Pew Internet Project's research related to mobile technology:

- 90% of American adults have a cell phone.
- 58% of American adults have a smartphone.
- 32% of American adults own an e-reader.
- 42% of American adults own a tablet computer.
- 67% of cell owners find themselves checking their phone for messages, alerts, or calls – even when they don't notice their phone ringing or vibrating.
- 44% of cell owners have slept with their phone next to their bed because they wanted to make sure they did not miss any calls, text messages, or other updates during the night.
- 29% of cell owners describe their cell phone as "something they can't imagine living without."

Data as of January 2014

Smartphone owners in 2014

Among adults, the % who have a smartphone

	Have a smartphone phone
All adults	58%
Sex	
a Men	61
b Women	57
Race/ethnicity*	
a White	53
b African-American	59
c Hispanic	61[a]
Age group	
a 18-29	83[bcd]
b 30-49	74[cd]
c 50-64	49[d]
d 65+	19
Education level	
a High school grad or less	44
b Some college	67[a]
c College+	71[a]
Household income	
a Less than $30,000/yr	47
b $30,000-$49,999	53
c $50,000-$74,999	61[a]
d $75,000+	81[abc]
Community type	
a Urban	64[c]
b Suburban	60[c]
c Rural	43

Source: Pew Research Center Internet Project Survey, January 9-12, 2014. N=1,006 adults.
Note: Percentages marked with a superscript letter (e.g., [a]) indicate a statistically significant difference between that row and the row designated by that superscript letter, among categories of each demographic characteristic (e.g., age).
* The results for race/ethnicity are based off a combined sample from two weekly omnibus surveys, January 9-12 and January 23-26, 2014. The combined total n for these surveys was 2,006; n=1,421 for whites, n=197 for African-Americans, and n=236 for Hispanics.

PEW RESEARCH CENTER

Statistics & Data
Cell Internet Access:

63% of adult cell owners use their phones to go online as of May 2013

34% of cell internet users go online <u>mostly</u> using their phones, and not using some other device such as a desktop or laptop computer.

How Americans Use Their Cell Phones (Activities):

Some 55% of cell phone owners say they use their phones to go online – to browse the Internet, exchange emails, or download apps. We asked them if they experience slow download speeds that prevent things from loading as quickly as they would like:

• 77% of cell internet users say they experience slow download speeds that prevent things from loading as quickly as they would like

• Of those cell internet users, 46% face slow download speeds weekly or more frequently.

Cell phone activities
The % of cell phone owners who use their cell phone to...

81	send or receive text messages
60	access the internet
52	send or receive email
50	download apps
49	get directions, recommendations, or other location-based information
48	listen to music
21	participate in a video call or video chat
8	"check in" or share your location

Source: Pew Research Center's Internet & American Life Project Spring Tracking Survey, April 17 – May 19, 2013. N=2,076 cell phone owners. Interviews were conducted in English and Spanish and on landline and cell phones. The margin of error for results based on all cell phone owners is +/- 2.4 percentage points.

(See: http://pewinternet.org/Reports/2013/Cell-Activities.aspx)

An April 2012 survey finds that some 70% of all cell phone owners and 86% of smartphone owners have used their phones in the previous 30 days to perform at least one of the following activity labeled as the "just in time" cell users:

- Coordinate a meeting or get-together – 41% of cell phone owners have done this in the past 30 days.
- Solve an unexpected problem that they or someone else had encountered – 35% have used their phones to do this in the past 30 days.
- Decide whether to visit a business, such as a restaurant – 30% have used their phone to do this in the past 30 days.
- Find information to help settle an argument they were having – 27% have used their phone to get information for that reason in the past 30 days.
- Look up a score of a sporting event – 23% have used their phone to do that in the past 30 days.
- Get up-to-the-minute traffic or public transit information to find the fastest way to get somewhere – 20% have used their phone to get that kind of information in the past 30 days.
- Get help in an emergency situation – 19% have used their phone to do that in the past 30 days.
- Overall, these "just-in-time" cell users – defined as anyone who has done one or more of the above activities using their phone in the preceding 30 days – amount to 62% of the entire adult population.
- 9% of adults have texted a charitable donation from their mobile phone. Mobile giving played an especially prominent role during the aftermath of the January 2010 Haiti earthquake, as individual donors contributed an estimated $43 million to the assistance and reconstruction efforts using the text messaging feature on their cell phones.
- The first-ever, in-depth study on mobile donors – which analyzed the "Text to Haiti" campaign after the 2010 earthquake – finds that these contributions were often spur-of-the-moment decisions that spread virally through friend networks.

Statistics & Data

- 74% of Haiti text donors say that their donation to the Haiti earthquake relief was the first time they had used their phone's text messaging function to make a donation to an event, cause or organization.

- 22% had texted a donation of some kind prior to their contribution to Haiti earthquake relief.

Cell owners in 2014

Among adults, the % who have a cell phone

	Have a cell phone
All adults	90%
Sex	
a Men	93[b]
b Women	88
Race/ethnicity*	
a White	90
b African-American	90
c Hispanic	92
Age group	
a 18-29	98[cd]
b 30-49	97[cd]
c 50-64	88[d]
d 65+	74
Education level	
a High school grad or less	87
b Some college	93[a]
c College+	93[a]
Household income	
a Less than $30,000/yr	84
b $30,000-$49,999	90
c $50,000-$74,999	99[ab]
d $75,000+	98[ab]
Community type	
a Urban	88
b Suburban	92
c Rural	88

Source, Pew Research Center Internet Project Survey, January 9-12, 2014. N=1,006 adults.
Note: Percentages marked with a superscript letter (e.g., [a]) indicate a statistically significant difference between that row and the row designated by that superscript letter, among categories of each demographic characteristic (e.g., age).
* The results for race/ethnicity are based off a combined sample from two weekly omnibus surveys, January 9-12 and January 23-26, 2014. The combined total n for these surveys was 2,008; n=1,421 for whites, n=197 for African-Americans, and n=236 for Hispanics.

PEW RESEARCH CENTER

CHAPTER 9:
Social Media

Let us look at more colors -- the tools - you could be using.

Why Use Social Media?

By becoming active and involved in the social community, it builds your brand and reputation while connecting with *your customers*!

Gary Vaynerchuk shares a shocking perspective about the businesses that failed to recognize and understand the ROI of Social Media. "...Borders didn't believe in it, they gave Amazon the infrastructure; they're out of business. Blockbuster didn't believe in it, they let Netflix come in and put them out of business."

Why Social Media Is Worth Your Time –
Let's Look At Obama's Use Of Social Media

Sometimes, one has to reach outside of their comfort zone in order to get what they want, and that's exactly what Obama did when he agreed to make a guest appearance on *Between Two Ferns*, a comedy podcast show starring Zach Galifianakis.
(Source and video found at: http://FunnyOrDie.com/m/8omu)

President Obama's appearance on a comedy show was part of his effort to spread the ideas of ObamaCare to a younger audience and his plan worked. The interview only lasted 6 and a half minutes, but it made the impact on the younger population that President Obama was aiming for. He had mentally prepared himself for the "edgy" questions he would have to face on the comedy show and he was willing to take the risk.

The United States is beginning to mold into how it used to be back in the roarin' 20's. Before the Great Depression, comedy, entertainment, and fun were growing exponentially. The Great Depression sent the United States into a slump, but now we have fully recovered and reached the point we used to be at during the 20's. The world has resorted to the way it used to be: filled with comedy, entertainment,

Social Media

and fun. Obama noticed this and came to the conclusion that to reach the audience of this new, fun generation, he would have to become a part of the hype.

The lives of the younger generation of the United States are focused around social media and entertainment. Everyone is searching for a good laugh, and the people of the new generation tend to respect those who they can laugh at. Take, for example, Jennifer Lawrence. She is seen as the female comedy idol of Hollywood and many young people look up to her for that very reason. Now take into consideration YouTube comedy stars like Jenna Marbles and Shane Dawson. Even though their humor is crude, they are widely respected and widely known across the world.

Obama took, perhaps, the ultimate plunge for a president, and even though he participated in a show that generally has an edgy genre of humor, his respectability has remained intact, and he has reached a broader crowd.

Social media is just another tool. It is new technology and it is not going away!

What is the Return on Investment (ROI)? There is lots of data to support the importance of social media – when used correctly and as part of a 360 degree plan.

Using Twitter or Facebook alone will bring you little to no sales. However, if you use social media as a means to interact and build a reader base, as one channel of your entire author platform, you may be pleasantly surprised. Twitter may not get you an immediate ROI (return on investment) but it will get you ATTENTION when used properly!

Which Social Channel Do You Like Best?

Each social channel is different, structured to appeal to certain traits, such as:
- Community
- Belonging
- Discussing topics of interest
- Sharing personal moments (births, children milestones)
- And yes, selling your *brand*.

Facebook is by far easier for different generations to use, because it's easy to read and understand it. You create your Facebook account, you speak in normal speech, and you interact. Parents and grandparents are on Facebook.

Henry Ford Didn't Listen To His Customers and Facebook Shouldn't Either
By Jennifer Grigg (Twitter.com/TheSocialDragon)

I quickly learned, there is no magic formula to beating Facebook. After all, why should we? We are using their platform for free to get out our business message. Sooner or later, free had to stop. Right?

It was devastating to watch a post on a client's page go from on average having 320 people see the post to only 50 seeing it. That's when I decided to take a closer look at what exactly was happening.

From what I noticed, Facebook probably did a good thing to start declining organic reach and making businesses pay to reach their audience. Yes, you can still reach your audience organically (or in other words, free) but if you want to reach a larger number of your audience, then you must pay. It's all based on budget, so it is still very reasonably priced. The reason why I said Facebook did a good thing, because it is just one step in the evolution of social media. Remember, if

Social Media

Henry Ford listened to his customers, he would have invented a faster horse, not an automobile.

There really is a lot of noise on Facebook. So many businesses are there, spilling their messages to everyone. From now on, to get past the noise and make our audience stop to pay attention, we need to be better than mediocre. Better than average. Better than our competition. We need to put out messages that showcase we ARE the expert in our industry. We cannot just do this once this week and maybe post in three weeks. We need to consistently on a regular basis be posting outstanding material that is ALWAYS relevant to our audience. No longer can your Facebook page be filled with motivational quotes and nothing else. More than ever, your Facebook page needs content...quality content...all the time! Test what works. I'm noticing posts that are text based seem to be getting more engagement. A text based post can include a link.

Now is the opportunity to streamline our marketing efforts. Blogging will be more important than ever before. We should be creating relevant posts on Facebook and linking people back to our websites, to our services, to our blogs, and to other social media accounts. It will take a bit of strategy, but we should, now more than ever, think what does our audience want from us? What makes them buy from us? Facebook was never meant to replace your website. If your business does not have a website and you only use Facebook as a way to reach your audience, you will need to rethink that.

I've heard people say "Well, if Facebook is making me pay for what was organic reach then I'm not going to use it anymore." With that, I say, don't stop using Facebook yet. Facebook is still the most popular social media platform out there and we need to continue to be where our audience is. Perhaps by the end of 2014, another social media platform will become popular. Or perhaps other social media platforms will watch what Facebook is doing and decline their organic reach too. It's too hard to predict right now.

So before you decide to remove yourself from Facebook, ask yourself how can you improve your branding to your audience. Take note to see whether or not Facebook was working for your business.

How often were you using Facebook? If you were not consistently using Facebook on a regular basis before, chances are it wasn't working for you. Not because your product or service wasn't great, but because you weren't putting in the effort.

Times have changed and we need to stop pushing our sales on our customers and taking them for granted that they will buy our product. Instead we need to interact with them, connect with them and build relationships that show we care about our products, our values and most importantly, we care about our customers. It is then, we will gain our customer's trust, and they will buy from us when they are ready.

2-Step Communication Tip

Do not just assume everyone communicates the same way YOU do. If you prefer voicemail but someone else prefers text or e-mail, oblige them.

Also, be sure to use a 2-Step method. If you leave a voicemail for someone, also text them, "When you get a chance, listen to the message I left you about ____."

If you e-mail someone, follow up with a phone call or text, "I'm just confirming that you received my e-mail regarding ____." This has tremendously increased the level of communication for all my clients and customers.

Twitter can seem like a big change to use for a business who has never used it.

Twitter has *following ratios*, #Hashtags, and @mentions (also called a handle). What is after the @ is called your handle or your Twitter ID. Those who are familiar with Twitter will know how to find you easily if you are *tweeting* often. Twitter also has a culture of reciprocity that doesn't seem to exist on other sites: I tweet you, you tweet me. I follow you, you follow me.

What is your Twitter handle?
My handle is @GoGlossy or @BusinessExpShow.

My hashtags are:
#ColorYourMessage or #RadioShow or #TBES.

Social Media

Here a hashtag for the Kasem Cares Foundation is #KasemCares. One can now easily search who is talking about #KasemCares when you type #KasemCares in the search bar in Twitter. It will give you a "feed" with many people who are "talking" about you. I like to think of it as an organized filing cabinet of hashtags. It is always a great way to follow other people or have them follow you by your own succinct various created hashtags.

Note: You cannot own a hashtag. Anyone can use it.

Twitter also has unfortunately become a way for people to spam links to their product or service, which goes against Twitter guidelines. You are considered spam "if your updates consist mainly of links, and not personal updates." (Source: https://support.twitter.com/articles/18311-the-twitter-rules#)

Writing Your Social Media Message

Be Authentic!

Do not make your messages all about you. Be original. Have your own voice and personal touch to your messages. It takes a long time to build up relationships with readers, bloggers, authors, and reviewers, which is ultimately your fan base. The point of doing all this is not to expect instant sales. You are building relationships and credibility that will hopefully result in word of mouth recommendations and sales.

Instagram

"The primary reason brands take to Instagram, is to create a 'community and culture' channel, in which brands show what it is like working at their companies." – Hubspot

It is no surprise that Instagram is so popular for both brands and consumers. Hubspot reports that 40% of people respond to visual content versus written and videos generate 3x the amount of inbound links than written posts.

Instagrammers are using hashtags in video sharing to promote favorites, contests, and to make posts more searchable with keywords. With that said, brands can formulate a more specific setting for their fans to share photos, giving themselves the upper hand with a ton of user generated content.

Instagram Quick Tips

- **Complete your profile**. Do not skip any steps. Be sure to link to other social sites and your website.
- **Interact.** Find users that are talking about your business or related fields. Follow and comment.
- **Be visible**. Show off your products, introduce employees, and show behind the scenes.
- **Be personable**. Engage with users as actual people with personality. People want to connect with brands that seem human.

Social Media

- **Use hashtags**. Instagram searches use hashtags, so if you do not tag your content, it pretty much hits a dead end beyond your followers.
- **Regram.** If you like a photo from another user – show them and *regram* the photo.

Never Run Out Of Messages – 27 Social Media Ideas
Contributed by Alyssa Ortiz

What's the hardest part of using social media for your business or organization? If you're like most small business owners, coming up with content is at the top of your list.

Here are sample ideas you can integrate into your business social media. You can use this in Instagram, Twitter, or your favorite social media outlets.

Create a photo challenge. Depending upon your business, you can use a little bit of business and little bit of personal.

1. **What Did You Do Today?** Use a photo of you (day in the life). *For me it was a photo depicting my radio life on-air.* Describe a day at work and how much you love it using ideas, but not quotes, from your product or service.

2. **Someone That Makes You Happy.** This is a personal one. *I used my son, Trey, to describe the importance of family in success since this is a common idea. We also emphasized the importance of kids learning business early.*

3. **Proud.** Use your notable photos (i.e. graduation) or award or a picture that represents your success.

4. **Somewhere You Went.** Use the most beautiful picture(s) you have of you somewhere to emphasize the places success can take you.

5. **Memory.** Use an old picture of you (i.e. Grandma's house) to emphasize your roots, as well as, foreshadow mentioning your story to show who you are.

6. **Motivation.** Use a photo with a motivational quote that you look to when you think of hard work and success.

7. **Technology.** Use a photo of your favorite technology and how it affects your business.

8. **Your Nationality/Ethnicity.** To show your diversity, you may want to emphasize this in your product/brand.

9. **Something I Made.** What cool art or hobby do you do? *As an example, I include a photo of my art.* Make it a point to show that you have a fun life outside your work.

10. **Highlight Of Your Month.** You can flashback to an event, conference or person you met.

11. **Inspiring Person.** Who is your role model?

12. **Post A Quote.** Include a graphic and hashtag #Quote #Inspiration

13. **My Favorite Tool.** You can get creative with this one, it can be technology, product or service that makes your job easier.) *For this book, we used a paintbrush to emphasize "Color Your Message."*

14. **Changes To Come.** What new ideas, products, or services are in your business?

15. **My Favorite Food.** Self-explanatory.

16. **My Favorite Book.** Just post a picture of your favorite book and maybe a coffee next to it, we have to make these photos catchy, not just random photos.

17. **Home.** Where are you from? Great way to reconnect and grow your social media brand on a personal level. *For me, I often show Texas and a little bit about my past.*

18. **Quiet.** A relaxing moment when you take time away from busy day-to-day life.

19. **Goal Of The Day.** Today I will edit 10 pages of my book.

20. **Gratitude.** Who are you thankful for? What should you show gratitude for?

21. **Best Part Of My Day.** Sum it up for your followers in text, photo, or a video.

22. **Dressed To Impress.** Business photo of yourself.

23. **Website.** Snapshot of a page on your website. Get us to go to your site!

24. **My Plan.** A chart of your daily plan for success.

25. **WOW!** Something business related that causes a big wow.

26. **Reward.** Something you find rewarding.

27. **Inspiration.** Talk about, retweet, or repost people who inspire you.

CHAPTER 10:
Hashtag Rising, Facebook Already There

We wrote an original jingle about our little friend hashtag.

(Sung to the tune of Twinkle Twinkle Little Star)

Hashtag, hashtag. Next to star.
Now I wonder what you are.
Used to be the number sign.
Press to dis-con-nect the line.
Now you're hashtag superstar.
Still - I - don't - know - what - you - are.

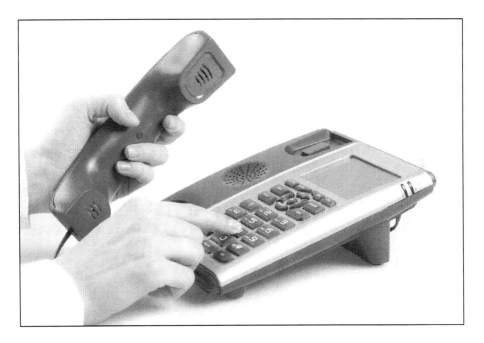

First posted on Twitter in 2007 as a way to identify groups on the new social site, hashtags are now used – for good or for ill – across nearly all social media platforms. There are now roughly 100 million active Twitter users (those who log in at least once per day).

- 40% of Twitter users rarely post anything, but primarily consume content there.

Hashtag Rising, Facebook Already There

- 55% access Twitter via a mobile device.
- Half of all Twitter users use the service to share links to news stories.
- Half retweet others.

The one word I use to describe a hashtag is *category*. It is all around us, you see it on television, hear it on radio, see it on many marketing pieces. A #hashtag is a word or phrase prefixed with a # that is commonly used to label a status update or photo. The hashtag is then searchable so you can find all posts with that hashtag, for instance: #ColorYourMessage.

So if hashtag is a category, in what categories would you like your messages to be found when someone searches for it on social media sites that use hashtags?

Specific social sites use hashtags, others do not. Popular ones are Twitter, Facebook, Google Plus, Tumblr, and Instagram.
You can use these hashtags for information and searching to find for example: coupons or a category of information.

As a business, hashtags are great way to see what people are posting about. It can be something specific about your business (i.e. #CraftBeers and #OldTownOrange for a restaurant client) or about related information (#BestView #SportsBar #HappyHour #HotDogs).

Browsing through hashtags on Instagram, you can see people's pictures and also other's comments. You can see what items are popular, what is trending, and generally whether sentiment is positive or negative.

Prior to hashtags in Facebook, the only way it was possible to see what someone was posting was if you were their Facebook friend. A Facebook search did not surface any functionality to let you "eavesdrop" on what folks were saying, so the addition of hashtags is very popular. Now you can type or click a hashtag and it brings up recent Facebook posts with that hashtag, assuming the person's privacy settings allow the post to be visible.

When you think about how you can best use keywords on Twitter for social media and hashtags, what you really need to think about is the audience you are appealing to. You also have to know the difference between trends, keywords, and the best use of hashtags.

Twitter lets you send out short messages, limited to 140 characters. These are called Tweets.

Hashtag Benefits:

- **Building hype.** Bring awareness to a subject, product or service. #MomBlogger #Author
- **Trend setting.** Get people talking and exchanging ideas about a particular topic. For instance, #Toy4Less or #YasGaga can be meme on Twitter.
- **Join in** on other people's hashtag trends and try to be funny and original.
- **Eavesdropping.** Listen in on conversations about your industry, product, or competition.

Hashtag Cons:

- **Overusing Hashtags.** There is a funny skit by Jimmy Fallon and Justin Timberlake describing what it would be like if we spoke in hashtag. I posted the video on my blog at: http://wp.me/p2BAqb-g0
- **Tag hijacking.** This happens when a brand or individual introduces a hashtag for one purpose and users turn it into a joke.
- **Doing it wrong.** Hashtags should be used on social media sites and nowhere else.
- **Talking to people as a corporate entity** versus talking to people on Twitter as a person.
- **If you know you have got a somewhat mixed reputation**, think your hashtag choice through more carefully.

Hashtags should be used carefully, but when done right they can be – pound for pound – as valuable as any other social media tactic.

Hashtag Rising, Facebook Already There

1. The # sign before a word is a way of *tagging* the word for followers of a specific trend or to notify members of a group that there is a specific post for them to respond to. This is a common networking tool and may or may not be made up of keywords with a high rate of searches.

2. Become an authority. Google algorithms are set up to recognize valuable content. This means that if you use consistently related tags and they lead to valuable content, Google will use their algorithms to eventually recognize you as an authority in a subject area. Likewise, if you randomly use a hash tag on unrelated materials, you will be identified as someone who is not an authority.

3. Do not limit use of tags. Put related tags on all your material so anytime it is shared on Twitter it will already be tagged.

4. Do not just use Twitter for social media & hashtags. Engage your audience with real conversations so they do not see you as a spammer. More than that, they will begin to personalize your posts and direct more followers your way.

One example of a good Twitter campaign is for a retail business that experiences huge drops in business during certain times of the day, such as a restaurant. You can use a Tweet as an instant coupon, to drive traffic to your business.

> Unadvertised Special – Say secret word ELF for 20% off today 2-4pm only @CoffeeHouse #SpecialDeal #UnadvertisedSpecial #HappyHour

This is a good way to drive traffic instantly. However, it will take time to get a following and then prompt them into action with your Tweets.

Be careful, because too many specials at regular intervals will condition your customers to wait for special deals only. Use this method randomly and sparingly.

This is Advanced Hashtagging with a purpose.

To Facebook Or Not To Facebook, That Is The Question

One of the big questions in business marketing is – what is the value of using Facebook?

Think of it as the modern day *word of mouth.* Facebook works well for some industries and some age groups.

Here is an image promoting the lifestyle of a business – posts today tend to be more favorable than those of yesteryear. If you post a photo versus simple text, you can add value to your one image by including your website or hashtag with your photo.

"Should I pay for Facebook ads?" It depends! For as little as $5 you can get your post seen by thousands of people. Experiment with Facebook, target your audience. The number of impressions you can get are enormous versus not paying to boost your ad.

This "Beer Brat" post is an example of what a $5 boosted ad can do for you. 928 people were reached. That means 928 impressions were made as one scrolled by this ad on their mobile device or computer. In comparison, not "boosting your ad," will get this client – based on their current following, on average of around 75 impressions. The result is more than 10x visibility. Would you pay $5 to do that?

Now, imagine if you paid $10 or more on an important event or day of the year, where you want to stand out. For the price of a cup of coffee, you can really stand out. Far cheaper than a freeway traffic billboard sign (and the black and white days).

Facebook aka "The Book Of Faces"

We spend *a lot of time* looking at pictures on the Internet. It is the killer feature that makes many of us keep our Facebook accounts active, quite frankly.

Users upload more than 250 billion images to Facebook alone, and we're continuing to upload them at a rate of more than 350 million per day.

Beyond the social networks, our search results are now permeated with images, too. Of the 3.5 billion searches that we perform each day, roughly 40% of the results list includes pictures inline.

The power of images has been directly tapped by several social networks over the past few years. The meteoric rise of Instagram and Pinterest are prime examples. Marketers have also been migrating towards these visual platforms as ways to reach more customers.
(Source: David Keyes, https://www.linkedin.com/pulse/article/20140929190800-21677256-the-one-reason-i-still-use-facebook-and-why-it-s-worth-20-billion)

Benefits Of Using Facebook

- People tend to trust their peers (word of mouth) over corporate advertising.
- Consumers stop following a brand on Facebook because the information it posted had become "too repetitive, boring and only has the brand in mind – not the user experience."
- It is a good way to send out positive messages about your brand or community involvement.
- It is a good way to stay in touch & reach masses of people.
- You can use Facebook as a website alone.

- When you do pay for a video inserted into your post, currently you can switch out your video link and change the message without paying extra for that. This is a really great feature!

Things I Am Not Fond About With Facebook

- Your Facebook content may not rank as high as other sources in web search results. You have to know where and how your customers are finding you. Are they searching on the web or see you as a result of a paid ad or because one of your loyal customers liked a Facebook post of yours?
- You will also need to monitor what your customers *and* employees say about your business if someone has access to your business Facebook or fan page. One wrong message, photo, or statement can put a dent on your reputation.
- Facebook can consume too much of your time. There are better colors that have way more benefit.
- A pay per ad campaign on Facebook could be rather costly as compared to using some other *tools*, such as video, which I will get into later. Also, it is not timeless, unless you keep paying for *ad boosts*. After you pay for a Facebook promotion, you cannot see it say a month from now at the top of your *wall* (unless you pay again). For your money there are better things, I personally would do – depending on your budget and industry.

Finally, if you are spending hours on end on Facebook versus running your company, you may want to think about outsourcing certain projects to your staff, intern or someone else to free up your time to focus on your business.

Hashtag Rising, Facebook Already There

According to Wikipedia:

Facebook (formerly Thefacebook) is an online social networking service headquartered in Menlo Park, California. Its website was launched on February 4, 2004, by Mark Zuckerberg with his college roommates and fellow Harvard University students Eduardo Saverin, Andrew McCollum, Dustin Moskovitz and Chris Hughes. The founders had initially limited the website's membership to Harvard students, but later expanded it to colleges in the Boston area, the Ivy League, and Stanford University..

CHAPTER 11:
The Wrong Color

One of the key ingredients I often see left out of social media marketing or advertising, is the actual involvement and relationship of the marketer or advertiser who is selling the business owner "the latest thing."

Someone tried recruiting me to work for his agency a few years ago AND did just that. He wanted to sell a *duplicable system* so he would not work as much!

What I kept seeing was wrong and the disconnect to the business owner is that he was not taking the time to understand:
- their brand
- what they know about technology
- what they don't know
- how many years they did do the right thing

He needed to take their message and use it to attract masses of people. He only cared about advertising for the client. He would sell banner ads, commercials, and pay-per-click. Banner ads would start at $12,000 for his campaign that got you x number of impressions.

Let me stop there. Have you clicked on a banner ad this year intentionally? I always ask this question and 95% of the time the answer is "No, I never click on those things. I know that it's spam or junk marketing."

I could not imagine selling such a high price campaign to a business just because it worked for you when you are asleep. Well, does it?

I argued with him that if a client of mine has $12,000 to spend on advertising or marketing, I would never steer them to banner advertising. Never! Do you know what I could do with $12,000? I could put them on a live radio show that gets broadcast to so many people on top of having messages and content that can be repurposed. Now, what has a greater reach and more powerful message?

The Wrong Color

> Doing business without advertising is like winking at a girl in the dark.
> You know what you are doing, but nobody else does.
> — Steuart H. Britt

There is a way to market for someone without ever being involved except collecting the order and cashing his/her check. Do you see how the message is lost? Do you see how the *colors* here are not used effectively?

Needless to say, after finding out many similar practices of his that just did not seem right, I quickly went on my own path of helping business owners the only way I know how: ***be involved***.

> *"I like being involved in interesting and creative things. I'd just rather be involved in creating it, rather than being in it."*
> – *Karen Gillan*

When interviewing the general manager of a car dealership about what was most important to him and his business, I asked what made his dealership different than other businesses? His response was "community." The dealership has a big community presence and customers come back time and time again, generation after generation, cousins, friends, local groups, etc. to bring referral business to their dealership. Also, Toyota of Whittier is not located – conveniently – off any freeway. To get to Whittier you have to drive about 4 miles or so inland.

So I took their word "community" back to our team and that started the basis of our involvement.

Be Involved And Make Things Happen

We decided that they needed to have a blog that would incorporate things they are doing and promoting their local messages to their community.

The first goal of theirs to be found "organically" via Google was using the words or phrase "oil change coupon Whittier." The owner said, "We don't come up on the top anywhere for oil change." Service departments for dealerships are important to bringing back customers and increase the longevity of cars for consumers using genuine parts.

Whittier Oil Change Toyota of Whittier Coupons ... - YouTube

www.youtube.com/watch?v=BKmh9RJdbt4
Nov 12, 2013 - Uploaded by Carmmunity
http://www.toyotaofwhittier.com/**service**.aspx **Oil Change** at
Toyota of **Whittier** Get Your Car or Truck Serviced ...

Car Specials Oil Change Toyota of Whittier Coupons Oil ...

www.youtube.com/watch?v=imnJBfEARwc
Nov 25, 2013 - Uploaded by Carmmunity
http://www.toyotaofwhittier.com/**service**.aspx Call 562-698-2591
Free Car Wash when you get your Oil ...

I was confident that in 3 or 4 weeks, we would have his business on the top pages of Google and YouTube doing our "magic."

Within about 10 days we got them to page 1 of Google and YouTube and used the YouTube Channel name "Carmmunity." Also, notice, would you most likely click on something on Google that has a photo versus text only? Another added value component. Why more companies in the 21st Century are not doing this is beyond me.

CHAPTER 12:
Content Is The New Black

Every business starts with an idea. Inspiring your team with proper content can significantly improve your brand. I invite you to get your key team players on board when developing your messages, brand, and content. The spiraling effect of having a team vision for your content can be innovative and have lasting results!

Forbes Magazine: "Content marketing is beginning to replace the term SEO."

Content Marketing

Most experts would agree that it is no longer enough to simply have an SEO strategy. In fact, I have noticed the term *content marketing* starting to become used synonymously with SEO. While the two should certainly be differentiated on many levels, many argue that content marketing is the 'new SEO.'
(Source: http://www.forbes.com/sites/jaysondemers/2014/04/30/the-top-7-seo-trends-dominating-2014)

There has never been a company that has handed me their *content* on a silver platter. That is okay – this is one of my favorite parts – writing and asking questions. It allows you to GET INVOLVED.

If you have been in business awhile, I promise you – you have lots of CONTENT! And if you need content – interview other people. Ask questions to people you want to learn from.

Content Is The New Black

These are the messages – this is part of your brand – it is why you started your business to begin with.

Again, content begins with: *What is your mission? What is your purpose?*

Everything these days needs proper content and messaging:

- Your Website
- Social Media
- Keywording (to get found via the major search engines)
- Blogs
- Tweets
- Verbal talking points

Written **content** probably got you to purchase *this book,* purchase other books, attend an event, or sign up for a course recently.

Become An Author

One day your compiled content can lead to a published book. Some of the content in this book started out by repeating messages from presentations, blogs, and verbal talking points to my customers. Your goal does not have to be to become a best-selling author – a book means you are a subject matter expert and:

- You Are Credible
- I Trust You
- You Like To Give Knowledge
- It Leaves A Legacy Of Your Greatest Work

I have easily generated tens of thousands of dollars in business from clients who chose business with my company over a competitor who did not have a published book.

Provide A Great Experience

Here are six essential elements your customer wants you to keep in mind from their point of view:

1. Know What I Want
2. Be Relevant
3. Be Knowledgeable
4. Be Dependable
5. Be Likable
6. Be Responsive

More Content Please – Why Content Marketing Is Valuable

The common denominator I find that CEO's and business owners need is *more content*! It is not enough for you to build a website and social media channels like Twitter, Facebook, Pinterest, and others. You need a 360 degree strategy that incorporates all the tools available to your business – many of them are free.

Incorporating content into a long-term strategy for your online presence is key. You want content and stories that are valuable to the reader, interesting, and shareable to allow you to capture and engage your audience.

I have helped CEOs and business owners retool their messages, speeches, and presentations into content for auxiliary outlets such as social media, blog articles, e-books, and radio messages. Retooling this information actually saves them time and gives a significant return on their resources.

Advertising

Why is it that major soda, fast food, or sports advertisers keep advertising the same thing or new content if they are so successful? Easy answer: Repetitive messages become subliminal marketing seeds to consumers.

To give you an example, here is TED speaker Ed Lesson about why we love repetition in music: http://youtu.be/1lo8EomDrwA.

I strongly believe the same thing applies for marketing: Looking back over the years at the radio ads we put out, we had the same consistent message on almost every ad. We had the same key points.

What Your Business Should Have In Place Before You Are Ready To Advertise

The following are factors and decisions to consider:

A manageable team. Assign who does what. Write or record job descriptions. Put your work in writing. If you had to be hospitalized or out for a week, would someone know where your data is? Would someone know how to "take over" and run your business? If not, how are you going to get there, to develop such systems?

Your business will be most effective and duplicable if you do all this. You cannot grow with one person trying to do it all. You cannot grow if you do not find a way to delegate and get reliable help.

Ask people in advance that you trust, "I'm forecasting my business growth. When I get busier, can I count on you to help me _____?"

Your personal and business budget worked out (and capital access if needed to fund your business growth). In other words, if you suddenly were to receive 5 or 10 times the business you get today, do you have systems in place to handle this growth?

Expectations of your proposed next 3 to 6 month's income stream.

A strategy or plan in writing.

Website. If you do not have a website, realize that it takes a few weeks to set this up. Before a website can take place, proper writing, content, photos, video and social media need to be in place. Do not take shortcuts. This loses time. And time is money for everyone around you or helping you.

Have multiple people help you with your "content." Do not try to go at it alone. Be willing to have a fresh perspective and critique. This is the time to implement what you do want changed or do not. "Innovation has been proven to lead to wealth."

Graphics. Do you have a logo and other printed materials on JPG, PNG, and PDF if necessary for online promotional needs?

Ask questions. Have you asked the right questions to get your business in order to go to the next level? What else do you need?

Help your marketing team. Create an order to your business that can then be translated into a marketing plan.

Timelines to help meet your goals. Do not try to do A through Z in one week or one month. It is likely impossible unless you have lots of working capital to pay a huge team. Instead, break down your goals into steps A through D, then E through L, and so forth.

Have reasonable expectations with regard to driving traffic to your site.

Content Is The New Black

Has Writing Lost Its Luster?
Your Content Can Make You Stand Out!

Writing is not exactly what it used to be. When it comes to creating content for the Internet or for other sources in today's world, it seems as though most writers are more focused on generating page views than creating content that actually touches and moves the reader. The problem with this type of thinking is that while it might generate a lot of page views, the question has to be asked regarding how many of those people that initially view the page are actually getting anything from the content located there. In fact, there is a decent chance that most of them are not even reading it.

When most people wrote in print media, they were required to write from the heart because the content that was in their stories had to reach a wide audience. Unfortunately, all of that changed when the Internet came along and people started writing for targeted audiences and virtually everything was online.

It seems now that people are more worried about including a specific word or phrase enough times to make sure that their page goes to the top of the search engine as opposed to touching any of the emotions that might be dwelling inside someone that reads it. This causes writing to become less of an art and more of a chore, both for the writer and for the reader.

The problem with writing from the heart is that most of the time, this content gets lost somewhere in the search engine and is never optimized, meaning that people that might be touched by it will never see it. Essentially, the only way to handle it is to learn to write for content and optimize the keywords or phrases and then make sure that the content has meaning and that it is able to move the people that read it.

This is very difficult because people that have been writing for quite some time often want to write what moves them and have little interest in writing for content optimization. By the same token, those that are adept at writing for content to make sure something gets to the top of the search engine often have a distinct lack of ability to write anything that is moving or meaningful. Combining both is very difficult and it is a skill that relatively few possess.

Some people write professionally while others only write as a part of their job description. The one thing that everyone has in common is that everyone writes something at some time. Learning to cut through all of the abstract information and get to the heart of the matter is something that everyone could benefit from and it may even bring writing back to the art form that it once was.

There are three things that can be done to help people who write to do a better job of reaching their audience.

1. **Ask Questions** – This helps the writer get in touch with his or her audience.
2. **Use Social Media** – Social platforms are here to stay and any writer that truly wants to reach the largest audience possible will utilize it to his or her advantage.
3. **Outsource Projects** – Sometimes writers simply do not have enough time to create great content for every subject. When necessary, outsourcing is perfectly acceptable as long as high quality standards are maintained.

Content Is The New Black
How to Connect With Generation C –
A New Formula for Marketing

What is *Generation C*? The *C* stands for *Content*, and anyone with even a tiny amount of creative talent can (and probably will) be part of this not-so-exclusive trend.

The Generation C phenomenon captures the avalanche of consumer generated 'content' that is building on the Web, adding tera-peta bytes of new text, images, audio, and video on an ongoing basis.

Sixty-five percent are under 35, but overall span the generations, empowered by technology to search out authentic content that they consume across all platforms and all screens, whenever and wherever they want.

They can be difficult to reach with traditional media – there is no one-size-fits-all solution here – but brands that take the time to understand them and properly engage with them will find a willing and influential audience.

Finding a way to connect with a new generation can seem like a daunting task. Learning how to mold your business around the latest generation's wants and needs is something that requires patience and perseverance.

Today many companies are faced with the challenge of marketing their goods and services to the new Generation C. This generation is often referred as the "social media" generation or the "YouTube" generation by many analysts.

This new demographic is changing the way many do business. Born on the internet, Generation C is the most socially connected and aware of all previous generations. Constantly plugged in, Generation C provides marketers with the perfect chance to reach them at all times. But many business owners and marketers, especially those of older generations, find it difficult to break into the social media world that drives this high tech generation. For those of you who are faced with this problem, here is some valuable information to help get you started in the new world of social media and content driven marketing.

Four great ways to make your marketing campaign enticing to Generation C:

1. **Shopping is now a social event.** In the past, when someone shopped online they just went to the website of their choice which was usually a major site like eBay or Amazon and completed their purchase. In today's world, for those in Generation C shopping has become social. Suggestions by friends and companies alike on social media platforms like Facebook and Twitter convince many to purchase a product. This follows the crowd kind of marketing words really well. So if you are going to market your goods or services to Generation C make sure to build and join social media platforms and make as many friends as possible.

2. **Content is king.** I know you have probably heard this phrase before because it is true. Only good content has a place in your marketing campaign. Many people in Generation C look to online sources for information. So if you are trying to market to this content-loving generation, you better have something useful to say. When adding content to your blog, website, or social media page try to add some useful and helpful information. This will help drive your marketing campaign and you will have a much better conversion rate.

3. **Web presence is important.** Statistics show that having a strong and authoritative online presence helps to draw in more traffic. Data shows that the more informative your company's website, the longer people will stay. This will lead to higher conversion rates for your marketing campaign and will help you retain more customers.

4. **Connect with this generation.** A great way to connect with this new demographic is to realize the fact that you are part of it. Yes, that is right, you! Just think about it for a minute. Do you spend time each day updating your Facebook page or other social media channel? How many times have you read the news online instead of watching it on TV or in a newspaper. The fact is many of us are part of Generation C including you and me. So if you are trying to connect with this new generation that most people are in, try to think of something that would attract you. Try to incorporate things in your marketing campaign that appeal to you and 9 times out of 10 it will appeal to other members of Generation C. Ask others from different age groups about their ideas and do not be afraid to have variations of marketing based on each generational gap so you target across a wide range of demographics and create new audiences – and essentially customers for life!

Content And Disruption

In 2011, my producer, Brian Gaps and I started a radio show called *The Business Experience Show*. This led to interviews of many amazing business owners! Some successful, some not. Some thriving, some struggling. Some startups, some 30-year businesses.

Their stories have been as diverse as could be. Sometimes you would not even think they were operating within the same economy. But they are. And the difference…their messaging.

When I think of the million dollars my business spent on advertising in the early 2000's compared to what is available today – for free – I just have to laugh.

The world has changed dramatically in the last five years. But the one thing no computer or robot, or app, can do is create messages or content for your business.

I cannot tell you how many businesses have people or bodies doing all the work and elements to run their business. The owner usually knows the business inside and out. However, ask them to put it on paper or ask them to give you their go to person who has such messages on paper, a blog, a website and time and time again, the businesses I encounter that need help – do not have such a person. So essentially we become that "ghost writer" for all their messages and branding.

If you do not have the discipline to write your own content because – let's face it, it takes uninterrupted time to do so and you are busy running your business – hire someone to do this for you. Outsource it. Stay focused on running your business and attracting more of what you love.

Your marketer should be asking you lots of questions, getting to know everything about your business, discussing what makes you and your business unique and competitive. This is part of a purposeful business relationship.

Whether I work with a small office or a corporate client, I pick your employee(s) brains and learn new things constantly and then develop compelling and useful information to make the public interested in your business. With that said, go back to your employees and ask them questions about their visions and let them take ownership in what they do for your business.

Messages and content are my favorite part of my work. I have not figured out why many people are afraid of writing the wrong thing, saying it wrong, or being blamed if it was communicated incorrectly. Having the initiative to put your brand, product, and service on paper, starting with sentences to build paragraphs is so important! Get a second or third opinion. Hire people who enjoy the art of writing.

There are many websites which do not have a company story, biography, or their hard working employees' bio information on their sites. Leave it to me to go in and change all that. Go ahead and disrupt the status quo. It is for the greater good. It is for your business to remain innovative and grow. It is for the people around you to see your business is staying fresh, relevant, and innovative.

Content Is The New Black

Here is a link to a great article by Forbes contributor Susan Gunelius entitled *5 Secrets to Use Storytelling for Brand Marketing Success*
http://www.forbes.com/sites/work-in-progress/2013/02/05/5-secrets-to-using-storytelling-for-brand-marketing-success

Love the game.

Love the game for the pure joy of accomplishment.

Love the game for everything it can teach you about yourself.

Love the game for the feeling of belonging to a group endeavoring to do its best.

Love the game for being involved in a team whose members can't wait to see you do your best.

Love the game for the challenge of working harder than you ever have at something and then harder than that.

Love the game because it takes all team members to give it life.

Love the game because at its best, the game tradition will include your contributions.

Love the game because you belong to a long line of fine athletes who have loved it. It is now your legacy.

Love the game so much that you will pass on your love of the game to another athlete who has seen your dedication, your work, your challenges, your triumphs... and then that athlete will, because of you, love the game.

– Unknown

CHAPTER 13:
Blogging

Blogging has become one of the greatest assets for SEO value. Google sees you more clearly and so do potential customers. If you have taken the time to clarify your brand up front, blogging will help refine it more. It can be simple paragraphs or photos or videos combined in any fashion, based on your preference and industry.

Ashley Torres (@PursuitOfShoes) was a CPA who, in her spare time, blogged about her love of shoes. Today she gets paid to blog about shoes! Her shoe blog is called PursuitOfShoes.com. You can find the link to her interview at the end of this book under the Chapter Resources & Links.

What is a blog? Here is an explainer video:
http://youtu.be/NjwUHXoi8lM

Blogging
blog
noun
1. a personal website or web page on which an individual records opinions, links to other sites, etc. on a regular basis.

verb
2. add new material to or regularly update a blog.

A blog (a truncation of the expression *web log*) is a discussion or informational site published on the Internet and consisting of entries ("posts") typically displayed in reverse chronological order (the most recent post appears first). Until 2009 blogs were usually the work of a single individual, occasionally of a small group, and often covered a single subject. (Source: Wikipedia)

Are you an expert in your field?

Are you using a blog in your business?

Do you work with outside vendors or community partnerships that you could talk about or feature in your blog?

Have you ever started a blog but it led to nothing so it is just there … sitting in the world wide web?

What is the reason one would want to have a blog?

Did you know that Google and other search engines seem to rank individual blog posts as websites? What do you think that does for your SEO value or for your web presence value? Tremendous value.

The images in your blog posts are one of the most important choices you can make to help promote that post. You can see it with visuals and images everywhere in social media. If you do not use images in your blog post, your chances of getting that post read go down to about 50 to 60%. Think about Facebook or Instagram and the posts that go into those timelines. There are always preview images that go along with those posts. Those interesting and eye-catching images are what get your attention so that you will look at the title.

The web has become more visual over the years. Think of Pinterest. It is a collection of images that links back to content that one finds interesting. Either it was an inspiring image or it was a product that you want to buy. It gets your attention (or not). Combine those images with hashtags and you can connect with other users looking for the same category. Twitter posts with images attached to them are three or four times more likely to be re-tweeted and shared than those without images. That is also why the images in your blog posts are so important.

(What is a hashtag? Read a blog post about it here.)

The Importance Of Blogging

Here are some important blogging points excerpted from a Craig McBreen article:
(Source: https://www.linkedin.com/pulse/article/20140728155645-27103281-your-startup-company-should-blog-here-are-4-big-reasons-why)

Your new company needs to start blogging, but there's a problem ...

Fear.

It is true. many organizations I work with have a fear of online marketing and it relates to cash. Mainly because *traditional* marketing *is* expensive.

You have probably done this. Hired someone to help with site design, copywriting, and overall branding, but paying a professional to build (and run) a long-term campaign? You do not want to make that investment, do you?

So, what *is* the answer? How does a lean startup get the word out without taking more risk than is needed or gambling away your hard-earned marketing budget?
How does a new company advertise and save money in the process? By building a blog.

Blogging

Google Will Find You.

River Pools is a company hit hard by the 2008 recession. They started blogging by answering customer questions. The questions were turned into posts built on honesty, filled with detail, and crafted with *long tail keywords*.

Mr. Sheridan's philosophy? "They Ask, You Answer."

River Pools and Spas was not a new company, but they were struggling and blogging changed everything. The site now dominates search in their industry and the company is thriving.

But here is the thing. This is a model your company can emulate and it might be what you need to get the search engine results you crave.

Here's how to start ...

a.) Bone up on long-tail keyword strategy. (See below)

b.) Take a close look at your business plan and begin your keyword plans there.

c.) Go through a <u>positioning</u> or <u>naming</u> or <u>tagline</u> exercise. You will be amazed how many topic ideas you might generate (even if you are happy with your current name or tagline).

d.) Use the River Pools methodology and think about specific questions your ideal customer might ask.

Next it is important for you to understand *long tail keywords*. These are search phrases, usually consisting of several words, that Internet users enter into search engines to find more narrowed search results about a particular subject, topic, or niche.

Short Tail Search = Ties
Medium Tail Search = Bow Ties
Long Tail Search = How To Tie A Bow Tie

There is a plethora of business to be had for any business willing to invest the time and content to target a wide variety of specific niche phrases related to their product or service.

Think of the 20 most prominent questions consumers ask regarding your product. These questions can form your titles for blog articles. Give your user valuable written content (with tagged photos or video included) and post regularly. At a minimum once a week, however twice a week is preferred for your blog's traffic to quickly skyrocket driven by its consumer-centric appeal.

Blogging Brings Your Brand Into Focus

Through blog entries, Google sees you more clearly and so do potential customers.

If you have taken the time to clarify your brand up front, blogging will help refine it more. This cannot be helped with the iterative nature of the process and trust me, this is good.

Your brand is constantly in motion. Each day you seek out new customers or prospects. You may have positioned your product or services like a master, but the more you write (blog) the more you will refine, like the artist spinning clay into a beautiful work of art.

You ... spinning, working, refining.

Blogging keeps the process in motion and in high-gear, which is great on so many levels. It is like creative juice for your brand.

Your ideal customer sees your product in a different light than your competitors. You are bringing something new and exciting to the world, just like your competition, but your competition does not have a blog. And even if they do have a blog, they might be going about it in the wrong way.

Blogging

A lot of people who are experts in their field post blogs about the ten most common mistakes in their field. Posting blogs with a number or bullet points can be very effective as people do get captured by useful nuggets that they can put into practice in their lives and that kind of thing.

Google constantly changes what ranks high in their search algorithms.

Many companies are finding the value and importance of blogging – and it is because it generates a wide variety of useful and relevant content.

Two of my favorite sites for creating blogs are WordPress & Blogger. Of the two, Blogger is more user friendly. WordPress requires a bit more skill or user understanding. You should choose your blog site based on your industry and your familiarity with technology.

Often times, we take over managing, adding creatively to, or completely creating a company's blog. This is called *ghost blogging*.

I know of a basketball coach who had never previously set up a website, much less a blog in his life. I asked him, "How did you learn how to do a WordPress site by yourself?" He said, "I don't have a budget to pay someone so I just learned by watching YouTube videos." Impressive, indeed. His blog website is 180Coaching.org. If you are a new business, you may want to save yourself some money and try this method.

Use Alt Text with Your Site's Images

In the code for each image on your website, there is a section known as *alt text*. This is the text that your website displays when it cannot load your images. It is also a big way that Google finds your website – by looking at the keywords in your alt text.

I often see website images that do not use alt text related to specific search terms. By using alt text with the search keywords you want to be found with, you will be able to ensure that you get found more often by people searching on Google.

5 Essentials For A Blogger

If you are a professional writer or blogger this is your business and in order to be successful you will have to implement marketing techniques that work. The fact is that blogging and writing is serious work and something you likely do because you love it. However, no one is a machine and from time to time will need a little help and motivation. In order to grow your business, you will have to implement best practices and ensure you stay up to date regarding the latest changes regarding content. The good news is that if you have the following five things, your writing or blogging career will be bound to take off.

1. ***Enjoy the art of writing***. Anyone can write. However, to write well and to create content that people are actually going to love, you should enjoy what you do. While you may not be passionate about every single topic you write on, liking what you do will help you get through these rather boring topics.

2. ***Write authentically***. If you are writing a blog, it is a good idea to write from your experience, what you know, and what you have done. The key to engaging content is to have your own voice. While you should try to provide an educational point to what you write, the key is to be relatable. The last thing you want to do is be too salesy, since this will simply turn off your readers and they will seek their content elsewhere.

3. ***Recruit help***. Writing is not a job you should go at alone. While you may be able to sit and brainstorm your ideas alone and put them down, it is essential that you have others read over your thoughts. This will include providing you with feedback, contributing new and fresh ideas, and editing the work when you are done. Not only will this help you cut down on the mistakes that you may have missed in your finished piece, it will also provide you with fresh insight about what you have written.

Blogging

4. *Discipline*. If you are writing as a job, you need to have a consistent time that you put aside to write. This can be each day, or each week, but the key here is consistency. In addition to writing, be sure you share your published pieces via social media. Let everyone know what you are doing. It is a good idea to do this at the same time each day, or week, as well.

5. *Stay knowledgeable*. As an entrepreneur you need to keep up with what is going on in your industry. This means attending conferences and seminars, reading on the subjects that you write about, and always staying up to date on new technologies offered in your industry.

The fact is that there are many people who do not realize the importance of blogging. It is where millions of people get answers and information each day. Embrace your talent and ensure you have the tools necessary to be successful.

Writing is a lonely business. Have colleagues to bounce questions off of, or to share your triumphs and challenges with. Don't try to go at it alone!

One of my most popular posts is about INNOVATION showcasing a YouTube video by Steven Johnson @StevenBJohnson with millions of views. He was a TED speaker and has written eight books including Where Good Ideas Come From: The Natural History of Innovation.

Most exhilarating is Johnson's conclusion that with today's tools and environment, radical innovation is extraordinarily accessible to those who know how to cultivate it. *Where Good Ideas Come From* is essential reading for anyone who wants to know how to come up with tomorrow's great ideas.

I wrote a related blog post contribution to endorse Steven's video and highly recommend it. Video and link sourced at: http://wp.me/p2BAqb-pv

7 Reasons Why Innovation Is Important

Innovation can be explained as the using of new ideas that lead to the making of any new products, services, or processes. Not only is the invention of something new important, but getting it out into the marketplace is just as important. This can involve management restructuring and technological transformation. Innovation means using new technology and using new ways of thinking to add value to an existing idea or product and to make substantial changes in society.

Studies have confirmed that businesses want to be more innovative. In my experience, *I found on average,* that almost 90% of businesses think innovation is a priority for their success. The importance of innovation is on the rise. Technology, digital trends and easy access to a plethora of information can help you build upon or complete your idea.

If you ask most CEOs, they will tell you that experimentation is imperative for their business. Experimentation is how new innovations are born and stay competitive. Automotive companies have concept cars; food companies experiment with new foods and flavors; retail companies experiment with placement of products and store atmosphere; drug companies are built on experimentation; tech companies experiment. Google Labs is a great example of innovation and experimentation. Take a look at sports teams – they experiment with new plays and players.

The different types of innovation that you are likely to run across include product, process, supply chain and marketing. The latter is the creation of new methods to market your product design or packaging with added enhancements.

So what are some of the reasons that businesses should use continual innovations?

1. *Creative Development*. Qualities of an innovative nature are essential for new businesses today. You can achieve growth by learning how to be creative. You need to learn this business skill to help make things of value from your creativeness. When you have this business skill you will find that it opens up all kinds of

opportunities and gives you the potential for a new market and helps you to keep up with the current trends.

2. ***Continuous Improvement***. Innovation gives organizational sustainability when you are making continual improvements and repackaging and re-branding. Any good manager will recognize the need to innovate and grows the business skills to increase their creativity.

3. ***Reinforce Your Brand***. Development branding is popular in organizational leadership. This process reveals information to help leaders to learn other ways to be more innovative. It is important because it is recognized as one of the main drivers for success. It gives organizational sustainability such as brand maintenance.

4. ***Making the Most of What You Have Already***. It is not all about creating a new product or service which you can sell, but you also need to focus on your existing business procedures to improve your efficiency, find new customers, increase your profits, and cut down on the amount of your waste. When you are continually innovating and improving on the practices of your business you will likely also attract better staff and keep more of your existing staff. This is beneficial to the health and performance of your business in the long-term.

5. ***Responding to Competition and Trends***. Innovation can help you see what exists now in the form of opportunities or be in alignment with ones that will pop up in the near future. Businesses which are successful do not only respond to the current needs of their customers, but usually predict the future trends and come up with an idea, service or product that can meet the future demand quickly and effectively. In this way you can stay ahead of your competition as trends, technology or markets shift.

6. ***Having a Unique Selling Point***. Generally, consumers will see innovation as something which adds value to products or a company. When this is used the right way, it can give you an advantage commercially, especially in a market that is saturated or shifting rapidly. It can get you more positive exposure in the media

and your customers will be more willing to pay the extra money for something that is well-designed and new, rather than picking the less exciting and cheaper rival.

7. *The Use of Social Media*. Including the use of social media in your innovation campaign is great for managing, motivating and getting focused in your business. When you use it in your business, you are drawing ideas from a wide range of people on the social networks, giving you a successful outlet to find new ideas for your business. You can also use social networks to see what customers are saying about your services, products or company.

In business today you must ask yourself if you need to become more innovative.

Do you feel the impact of globalization, technological and knowledge revolutions, migration, and climate change issues?

Innovation can bring the added value you need to your business plus widen your employment base. It may be beneficial for the quality and growth of your business.

Blogging

"Bill Gates (and Ray Ozzie, former Microsoft Chief Technology Officer) were famous for taking annual reading vacations. During the year they deliberately cultivated a stack of reading material–much of it unrelated to their day-to-day focus at Microsoft–and then they took off for a week or two and do a deep dive into the words they've stockpiled. By compressing their intake into a matter of days, they give new ideas additional opportunities to network among themselves, for the simple reason that it's easier to remember something that you read yesterday than it is to remember something you read six months ago."

CHAPTER 14:
Google Gaga

Google and the Google logo are registered trademarks of Google Inc. Used with permission.

Google covers 70% of online searches. "Let's Google it!"

If you are not communicating effectively and correctly with Google, then Google is going to ignore you.

Google is the 800-pound gorilla of online business marketing.

If you do not speak Google, you had better learn. And quickly. Google can seem complicated, but it is very important. At a minimum, it is worth spending hours and hours poking around. Way more important than hours spent on Facebook, although both are important on different levels.

Use Google!

- Look at what your content, listing, and links look like to new customers finding your business via **Google Search Engines**.
- Google Dashboard is a good place to find many of the assets available to you.
- Google Plus is a powerful networking place. Be sure to set home and work locations.
- Be sure to place you business on Google Maps.
- Google Places For Business is another listing area.
- Your **Google Reviews** are very important, please stay on top of them.
- Google Analytics should be integrated with your website.

Google Gaga

- Your website person should be integrating helpful Google Webmaster Tools
- A YouTube channel provides invaluable marketing opportunities via Video SEO, whatever your product or service (see chapter on Video)
- Research your industry Keywords
- **New services** and functions are constantly being added to the Google family, always be sure to explore the latest utility that you find
- Google offers a **free SEO guide** – simply Google it to find it – and Google will show you what to do

When you create your Google profile, Google will ask for your first and last name. *Do not* put the name of your company under first and last name. They can freeze your account for doing that. When it asks for a person's name, use a real person's name.

Be sure to verify your Google accounts with a telephone number or other method requested by Google.

Talking to Google is important, It wants you to speak to it in the language that Google understands.

People today are also confusing Google with multiple identities. You need to consolidate all of your Google tools to one account and disassociate other Gmails if you are using many to represent the same entity. (Do not feel bad – it happens. Even one of our major corporate clients ruined their Google account – it took us two months and lots of luck to unwind the mess that an inexperienced user created.)

Tip: You can use various browsers (Internet Explorer, Firefox, Chrome) to open various Google accounts at the same time.

Obviously Google is not the only game in town, as people use Bing, Siri, etc., but Google covers around 70% of it.

Another great free service is <u>Google Voice</u>. It is a convenient way to get a second phone line on your smartphone for business use.

Do you give out your personal cell phone for your business calls and clients? Did you know that Google Voice is free?

- It can transcribe voicemails and send the text to your phone.
- It can forward to any phone number you want.
- It also can forward your call to a free phone app or email.

1.4 million people have a Google Voice but do not actually use it.[*] I list my Google Voice on my business card versus putting my cell phone number. (Source: http://gizmodo.com/5395151)

"Successful people are simply those
with successful habits."

-Brian Tracy

CHAPTER 15:
Branding

You are your own brand! Every day, everywhere you go. Be inspirational and passionate in the messages you convey!

Your online reputation can impact virtually every aspect of your digital marketing. Controlling the conversation around your brand is critical to upholding and improving reputation.

We have all heard the phrase "Image is everything!"

The internet has a high demand for your photo. When someone googles your NAME – *what do they find*? Are the photos on your LinkedIn and Facebook done by a professional photographer?

Use a professional photo versus a candid snapshot. Invest the time, money, and effort into your brand. It makes a difference.

Branding

Here is an example of a before and after text only versus photo inserted into a Facebook post.

A photo has been shown to significantly get more likes than just written words in certain social media outlets.

The photos and visual images you post can have an influential part of your brand and how we will remember you long after we scroll by the post.

Grapevine Wine Shoppe Special Of The Week
15% off all champagne in store or online
Stock up for the holidays!!!
www.grapevinewineshoppe.com

Like   Comment   Share   👍38 💬 7

Like Comment Share   👍440 💬 38 ↗ 15

When it comes to your ***personal branding***, every activity is a potential photo opportunity. I take photos of nearly everything I attend in a professional capacity (networking events, association meetings, business luncheons, etc.).

I also take photos of fun personal activities. Occasional personal photos give potential customers another chance to relate and connect with me. These also spur content for my social media accounts.

But remember to be selective about what you put forth in your branding. I photograph a lot, but I post a modest amount.

> *Your smile is your logo, your personality is your business card, how you leave others feeling after having an experience with you becomes your trademark.*

10 Ways To Establish Yourself (or Your Brand) As A Thought Leader

Here is an article by LinkedIn influencer @DrewAHendricks
Source: http://www.inc.com/drew-hendricks/10-ways-to-establish-yourself-or-brand-as-a-thought-leader.html

The more your target market is exposed to your brand, the more the people in that market will recognize you as a thought leader, feel a connection, and buy from you. Here are a few tried-and-true strategies you can use to establish your expertise in your niche.

1. Publish Plenty of Free Content

Content can include:
- Guides
- Emails
- Blog Posts
- Videos
- E-Books
- Podcasts
- White Papers

The more valuable content you publish, the more you will establish your brand as an authority in your field. In an era of marketing, when people are being bombarded with content, they like value. If you give them something they can sink their teeth into for free-- such as an e-book--you can not only establish brand awareness and credibility but also add them to your email list, and then nudge them toward buying your products.

The more quality content you create, the better: 60 percent of marketers create *at least one* piece of new content each week.

2. Make It Dead Simple to Access

I am not a fan of sites that require you to give your email address, name, phone number, income, and children's first names (I'm slightly kidding on that last one) just to access some "free" content. It is not free if

Branding

visitors have to pay for it, either with money or the time it takes to input all that info. You can require an email address so you have them in your database, but even that is not necessary. If you are really driving value with your offering, they will come back for more. Here is an article on 5 Steps to Proper Conversion Rate Optimization with tips on how to analyze your marketing performance: http://blog.hostgator.com/2013/04/04/5-steps-to-proper-conversion-rate-optimization where the Web company HostGator provides an excellent resource for optimizing conversion rates by testing and simplifying the acquisition process.

3. Provide Value on Social Media

Here is what *not* to do on social: constantly send out links to your website, in the mad hope that people will click the link and buy something. Instead, consider yourself an indispensable resource. You have knowledge that others want. Share it by:

- Answering people's questions
- Joining in conversations
- Sharing relevant content (both yours and others')

Remember: **Thought leadership is about your audience members, not you.** They have problems, and you have advice that can help them. Social media is a great place to build relationships, but only if you keep helpful solutions in the foreground.

4. Guest Post on the Right Sites

Guest blogging can be useful as a thought leadership tool, but like everything, it can also be used incorrectly. Your goal here is to find popular, well-trafficked blogs that target the audience you are trying to reach. Then you need to find your unique voice as a guest blogger. What can you deliver that no other contributor has covered? What gaps can you fill in that will make you stand out? Are you writing for the write audience?

5. Tell Your Story

There's a reason storytelling is a trending concept right now. People identify with stories, not corporate branding messages. They want to know who you are as a person, so they can find connections to you. Maybe in addition to running your business, you are an avid World Cup fan. Or you have triplet daughters. These are little tidbits of your own life you might assume are better swept under the rug in your business life, but actually, whenever you can inject something personal into your message, you will instantly create rapport with your audience.

So go ahead, use your personal anecdotes in your blog posts. Share a tale in your email. Find ways to really personalize your business.

7. Write a Book

While you should not necessarily expect to end up on the *New York Times* bestseller list, writing a book (or two) is a great way to further establish your expertise. There is heavy clout around saying, "I'm an author," and with self-publication and digital books so prevalent, it is easy, too.

Do not fancy yourself as an author? Hire a ghostwriter. You can still get your knowledge and voice across, even if you do not have the time or skill to write it yourself.

8. Be Controversial

It is hard to stand out if your opinions are the same as everyone else's. And while it takes gumption, going against the current may net you more followers (and more customers) faster. Find your voice by challenging the status quo and bringing up points others have not thought of. But do not force it; if you cannot find a way to stand out by going against popular opinion, it will only come out as fake.

9. Speak at Every Opportunity

If the thought of speaking to a roomful of potential customers does not give you stage fright, give public speaking a try. By putting yourself in front of the right audiences at trade shows, conventions, and conferences, you further brand yourself as an expert in your field. If you have physical products or a book (see #7) you can sell afterward, most venues will permit it. Just stay true to your core message: What do you want to be known for? What topic do you want to brand yourself on? That is what your speaking engagements should cover.

10. Be Constant

If all this branding is succeeding at making you a known expert, you are probably going to be swamped with work. But do not let that derail you from continuing your branding efforts. You may need to hand some tasks over to others on your team so you can focus on your thought leadership efforts, but it is well worth it if it is slamming you with business.

Read more: http://www.inc.com/drew-hendricks/10-ways-to-establish-yourself-or-brand-as-a-thought-leader.html

CHAPTER 16:
Keywords

Keywords are the words and phrases that characterize and describe your product or service. These words are like breadcrumbs that can lead new customers to your business.

Search Engines rank these words with high importance. Therefore, you should make it a high priority to include these keywords within the body of your content when getting out your messages.

It is important to cover as many relevant keywords as possible with regard to your business. But be selective about quality, since many operatives limit keywords to as few as ten, sometimes even six.

How do you rank more than just a handful of keywords for your business?

You can use multiple videos, multiple blog posts, multiple landing pages, and relevant content to extend your keyword range beyond the customary limits.

Keywords

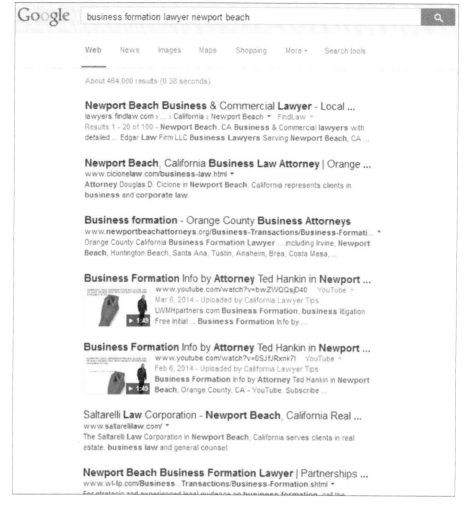

Another note about keywords that you can probably chalk this up to the popularity of the Siri app on iPhones, but getting found with your keywords has shifted to more conversational phrasing in the past year or so.

This was a component of changes made to Google last year. Keywords used to be fragments. They have now shifted to phrases, such as:

- Where can I find the best such and such?
- What is the best place to live in Los Angeles County?

Remember to keyword conversational phrases that a customer would use in finding your product to get found on search engines.

One Picture Is Worth A Thousand Words

An unused component of keywording, but one that I find to be very important in branding is the application of keywords to photos. Blog sites and other template websites often allow for keywords to be added when posting a photo. Sometimes this is called *alt text*.

It is very important for you to remember to keyword photographs, as they are a critical aspect of your content.

So few companies do this. One way to check your level of photo keywording is to search Google Images using your business name or industry keywords. This is also another way to move yourself ahead of your competition.

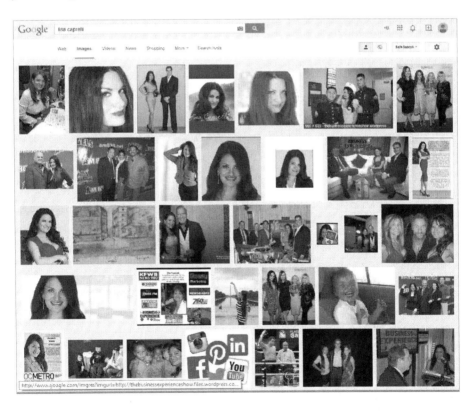

Keywords

Realize that having a website alone is different than a web presence. When you Google your business keywords, they are like breadcrumbs to help find your website – if done correctly..

Get your ACT together:

- Achieve your targeted keywords.
- Content is king!
- Target your audience.

**"We either make ourselves miserable
or we make ourselves strong.
The amount of work is the same."**
-Carlos Casteneda

CHAPTER 17:
Video

If I had to use only one color...if I had the marketing dollars to reuse all over again in the early 2000's over radio advertising, I would choose *video* ten times over. This is one of my favorite tools. I think this tool is so important that I designate it the color red.

Video allows companies to address customers as people, which helps tremendously to create a connection.

Under the umbrella of video there are great FREE tools and resources to help you get your message – your content – out to the public!

A third of all online activity is spent watching video and YouTube is the number two search engine. According to a report from Cisco, video is expected to grow to 84% of Web traffic in the U.S. by 2018, up from 78% this year. It is predicted that there will be more mobile-connected devices than there are people on earth!

If your brand does not have a video strategy, you are missing out on countless opportunities to build your brand and find new customers and audiences.

(Source: http://www.foxbusiness.com/industries/2014/06/10/cisco-videos-to-make-up-84-web-traffic-by-2018)

According to a Nielsen Cross Platform Media Study, Americans now consume an average of 60 hours of media content weekly and 47 hours (78%) of that content is video. Studies also show that 77% of TV viewers are using another device (mobile/handheld/laptop) simultaneously with television. This has created rapid changes from traditional video advertising.

Video

In a world of constant change, when it comes to attracting an audience, *short* and *worthwhile* are valuable. By focusing on your customers' daily needs and concerns, video marketing becomes your strongest asset. But with 100 hours of video being uploaded to YouTube *every minute*, 5 tweets *per second* containing a Vine link, 150 million users on Instagram and 675 million people tuning in to watch Vimeo videos – how do you break through the clutter?

Keep the connection with your audience by "including" them in community opportunities. Share presentations, clips from conferences, speaking or marketing events, and make them feel like they are part of what you are doing. Use video for interacting with viewers.

I have found that people are 8 to 10 times more likely to respond to you if you include a video.

According to Pew Research, 73% of online adults use social networking sites and 47% of them take photos or videos that they have found online and repost them on sites designed for sharing images with many people. This number grows increasingly each year!

Reposting videos is popular among Internet users ages 18 to 29. More than half of them repost videos. Millennials use social media to share and gain knowledge and give or receive feedback from friends and family, with Likes, Tweet and comments.

Advantages Of Video

- Engages the consumer, converts leads to sales
- Raw data, still photos and slide shows are not as powerful or engaging as a full motion video
- Save time during your customer's research and purchasing process
- Enhance their experience with video
- Builds trust and goodwill
- Provides instant access to information within video

You Want Your Customers To Feel They

- Got easy access to the information about your company or products (without being sold)
- Did not have to be pitched from a salesperson
- Can learn about your products and services – thereby cutting down the choosing you cycle
- Are in control of the experience in choosing you
- Boost their confidence
- Want to stay on *your website*, moving a sale forward until they are ready to buy

Tips

- Include your video on your website and landing pages
- Include your video in your e-mail marketing
- Include your videos in social media and Facebook posts
- You can re-purpose your videos

Types Of Videos To Consider Making

- **Explainer Videos**. These are short online videos used to explain your company's product or service. Explainer videos, often placed on a landing page, your website's home page, or a prominent product page, have become extremely popular – some sites boast of conversion rates increasing by as much as 144% after including an explainer video on their website. (http://www.invodo.com/resources/statistics)
- **Client Testimonial Video**. Build trust, community, and connection.
- **Question And Answer Video**. Get a professional or business coach to interview you on camera about the top lessons or tips your product or service offers.
- **Commercial Or Trailer Video**. The YouTube trailer is an opportunity to encourage viewers to click to subscribe to your channel. More subscribers means more views…which means more revenue if you have chosen to go that route with YouTube advertising. Aside from any financial reward, more viewers mean

more people being aware of your brand and what you do. It is now also common practice for traditional official movie, TV and games trailers to be featured on YouTube.

- **Storytelling Video**. Here is a YouTube video showing how SalesForce used the power of music, images and storytelling in their recent *How To Become A Customer Company* video. It is a great example of harnessing the full experiential power of video to tell a story: http://youtu.be/2wTE3k0GqTg
- More great tips on making a good video can be found at: http://www.mywebpresenters.com/articles/2013/10/make-great-youtube-trailer-video

Promote Your Videos

Publicize your videos and your channel on the radio, TV, websites, forums, newsletters, other social networking platforms. Link your video channel in as many places as you can: websites, blogs, magazines.

Allow **embedding** so others can distribute for you. Use the embed URL that comes with each video to embed your videos on your website. Send the links to blogs which may want to display your content.

Engage Your Audience

- **Don't Be Shy**: Speak directly to YouTube community and ask them to subscribe!
- Use **Video Descriptions and Banners** to encourage users to Like and Subscribe.
- Enable **Comments** on Video Pages (remember you can always delete comments or block users).
- Use **Playlists** to group your content by theme – this makes it easier for users to find videos on your channel.
- **Engage** your audience through shout outs, comments, subscriptions, and by asking questions or soliciting ideas.
- Encourage **Contests**. Use eye-catching titles in your videos.

You do not have to spend a fortune on doing a video to make it effective. Here is a video with tens of thousands of hits. This video was created for the AARP video contest and placed second. It is based on the Argentinian Political Advertisement "The Truth" by RECREAR: http://youtu.be/42E2fAWM6rA

Using video in search engines, websites, and blogs has a longer lasting impact than a radio ad that goes away after it is heard.

Video also has a high SEO value! Google loves video content.

In the book ***Online Video Revolution: How To Reinvent And Market Your Business Using Video***, author John Cecil says the web has gone from a text-based platform to a video based platform.

When we were interviewed guests on another radio show, my producer brought in our own video cameras to record the radio show on video. The hosts in the room looked at us and asked, "We need to start recording our own talks?" The answer was *yes* – doing so has an enormous value in your effort to create content.

More About YouTube

You should have a YouTube channel if your customers are watching videos related to your field. According to comScore:
- 90% of online shoppers find brand videos helpful when making a purchasing decision
- 65% of consumers will visit a brand's website after viewing a video to learn more.

It all depends on the industry, the content, and the goals you have for your business. I have been able to help turn businesses around using videos and content sharing sites like YouTube, Daily Motion, Vimeo, and Vine.

Video

Heard It Through The ~~Grape~~ Vine

Vine is one of the latest big video platforms. It is a mobile app that limits the user to 6-second video clips. Be fast, to the point, and fun.

"Brand Vines are shared 4x more than other online videos, and *5 Vines are shared every second on Twitter*," says Heather Taylor, vice-president at advertising behemoth Ogilvy.

Don't Forget To Use <u>Keywords</u>

Be consistent and put keywords in video descriptions, tags, and titles to improve search results. Always include a link to your site in the video description to improve traffic and SEO.

Many companies simply do not submit a URL or related description with their video. This is a costly mistake!

Google's algorithm seems to rank your site much higher in their search results if it contains video content than if it does not.

Before you publish your video: Proper encoding of title, description, and keywords will help your SEO more than you can imagine.

Worksheet For Gathering Key Information For Videos

What are the top 5 questions your customers ask?

1. _____

2. _____

3. _____

4. _____

5. _____

Consider your primary demographics:

Age group: _____

Income: MAP _____

Gender: _____

Ethnicity: _____

Marital status: _____

Psychographics of your customer:

Life style: _____

Social class: _____

Interests: _____

Activities: _____

Values: _____

Video

Key Questions To Consider

Who is your market?

_____

Where is your market?

_____

How much of your market would you like to reach?

_____

What would you like to accomplish with this campaign?

_____

What do you have in place now to start taking new customer orders?

_____

How many videos do you plan on distributing monthly?

_____

Are you directing traffic to your website or landing page(s)?

_____

Geographically, where would you like these videos to be seen?

_____

CHAPTER 18:
Public Relations

Publicity provides credibility and a much faster return. One prime national interview or news story can bring more response than an entire ad campaign. Just ask those who have been featured by CNN, Fox, *The Los Angeles Times*, *Good Morning America*, *Ellen*, *Oprah*, or *The Today Show*.

Publicity provides credibility and often a much faster return on investment than traditional advertising. One prime time national interview or news story can often generate a greater response than an entire ad campaign. Just ask those who have been featured on CNN, Fox News, *Good Morning America*, *Ellen*, *Oprah*, *The Today Show*, or in a major newspaper like *The Los Angeles Times*.

> *"If I were down to my last dollar, I'd spend it on PR."* – *commonly attributed to Bill Gates, Founder of Microsoft*

Public Relations (PR) is all about relationships. This field can help drive your business publicity via online and offline presence.

Not everyone needs PR. *Who needs public relations?* USA Today said, "Publicity is becoming like politics and people are realizing that fame does not happen accidentally." Working with a powerful and experienced publicist is the key. It is not just a job that involves sending out press releases.

Public Relations

Here are a few tips to easily increase the volume of your content marketing (when it comes to radio or media interviews):

Take out the sales pitch. Educate – don't sell. You know how your product or service can benefit others. Show them.

Digital Media can be *Multi-Purposed*. Use your radio or podcast show and turn it into an iTunes channel. You can take a 30-second radio ad, create a YouTube video for it, and cross-promote it on Google, Facebook, and your e-mail newsletters. There are so many more sharing opportunities in this regard.

Whatever you *find yourself talking about over and over again* – blog about it. *Write it down* and develop a finished story for your customers. Keeping it all in your head does no one any good. Your customers want you to share your knowledge and expertise.

Get your **interviews** transcribed and turn that into content.

To give you a better understanding of how the public relations process works, producer **Brian Gaps** and I interviewed **Tom Martin**, the founder and president of *Tom Martin Media, LLC*. Tom is a public relations and communications expert who has helped a wide range of individuals and companies receive wider media exposure. We frequently collaborate with Tom in connecting with media on a local as well as a national level.

Lisa: Tom, please tell us about your business background.

Tom: Prior to moving into the PR field, I spent 20 years as a television news producer -- and that meant producing stories for Diane Sawyer, Charlie Rose, and the late Charles Kuralt. Charles was the original host of CBS "Sunday Morning," and he had a very big impact on me. I've also worked as a producer with many other shows, networks and projects over the years -- producing restaurant stories for The Food Network, producing business news stories for The Nightly Business Report on PBS and for CNN financial news. The one fundamental insight that I gained from my work with all these shows and networks is that everyone has a story, and all human beings are just naturally fascinated by people with a story. These stories really spark our imagination in a powerful way. Eight or nine years ago, when I reached the twenty-year point of my television news career, I decided to move over, to "the other side of the line," to work in the field of public relations. I've always thought of myself as a storyteller – whether I was telling those stories as a member of the news media or as a publicist, on behalf of a client. Sometimes people need a little structure and help in communicating their story and their message in a powerful and effective way, and I sort of think of myself as the bridge that helps a client make that happen. When someone has a message they really want to deliver to a larger audience, I love helping them do that, because I know how satisfying it feels to be heard, when we have an opportunity to share our wisdom with others. I think this desire to communicate with others is a fundamental and natural human desire, and I love helping people do this. Whether I'm on the news side of things or on the PR side, that's how I see my role.

Lisa: It sounds like you must have worked very hard during your news career. I'm sure it didn't come easy. How did you get your start? Did you start as a writer?

Tom: When I first began my career in the news business, my title was that of "assistant producer" which was basically the lowest rung on the ladder in the newsroom. After paying my dues in that role for a few years, I had the opportunity to move up the ladder to the position of "associate producer," and so on. When I went to college in Washington, DC in the early 1980s, my plan was to become a lawyer like many friends of mine. After working part-time for a couple of law firms there in Washington, I quickly realized that this was not really the path for me, after all. As a result, during my senior year of college – as I was wondering what new path I might want to explore -- a friend of the family helped me land a job on the assignment desk of the CBS News Washington bureau. This job involved helping the CBS News correspondents who

covered the White House, faxing scripts from producers to correspondents and news anchors (for those of you who remember "faxing"), and this job also often meant running over to one of the Senate office buildings on Capitol Hill to interview a Senator, or something like that. I was really just helping out here and there, as best I could. If you ever saw the movie "Broadcast News" starring Holly Hunter and William Hurt, that film gives you a perfect sense of what the CBS News Washington bureau was like at that time. My friend Susan Zirinsky, who was working there as the bureau's White House producer at that time, served as the role model for the Holly Hunter character in that film – and they even look remarkably similar.

This was in the mid to late 80's, and Charlie Rose had just been named host of a new show called "Night Watch," which was broadcast in the middle of the night on CBS News back in the days before there were 500 different channels for us to choose from. I had a chance to move from working on the assignment desk to a position producing interviews for Charlie, which was a lot of fun. Aside from the countless politicians there in Washington, I produced interviews with sports figures, writers, musicians and many other interesting characters. It was a lot of fun, and a great experience. Almost always, we did our interviews at a studio right there in Washington, but one time I did have a chance to go on the road with Charlie Rose, to produce two interviews in Las Vegas – with Julio Iglesias and the comedian Dom Deluise – while Charlie was en route to California, to do an award-winning interview with the serial killer Charles Manson. That's the news business for you, switching gears from Julio Iglesias to Charles Manson!

In terms of my work as a writer, when I was working in the news business, the writing I did was often preparing briefing packets and suggested questions for an on-air anchor like Charlie Rose, Bryant Gumbel, or Diane Sawyer. In my work for shows like CBS "Sunday Morning" and "Good Morning America," I often wrote scripts for video segments, which always felt like producing a "mini-documentary," trying to put as much information and content into a video segment as possible, while still keeping it entertaining and engaging. As a result, I do think of myself as a storyteller, whether that means writing or working with a camera crew, or playing a supporting role to an on-air correspondent or news anchor, or helping a client make the most of an interview opportunity.

Lisa: It sounds like you've worked on a very wide range of stories. Would you say that you gravitate toward human interest stories?

Tom: Yes, I would say that I do. When I was producing stories for CBS "Sunday Morning" and "Good Morning America," I definitely had a preference for human interest stories. I loved asking people questions like, "What are you most passionate about?" It's funny, because back in the years when I was producing interviews for Charlie Rose, I can remember being there in the control room with the director. During just about every interview that Charlie did, we were always waiting for the point in each interview

Public Relations

when he would ask his "signature question" – "Can you give me a sense of the magic of your craft?" It might sound a little ridiculous to phrase the question like that, but I really do love talking to people and getting them to share the "nuggets of wisdom" that explain why they do what they do. I spent three years producing restaurant stories for The Food Network, and you might think that kind of assignment would get a little repetitive after a while, but I discovered that every chef and every restaurant owner has a unique vision and a slightly different way of doing things. For example, when I was interviewing each chef and restaurant owner, I might ask, "Are you trying to be an artist?" And I might ask them, "What were the obstacles you faced along the way, as you were pursuing your dream?" I love stories that have real integrity, where someone is eager to tell their story with the intention of really helping others. We all have dreams and goals, and we all encounter obstacles and challenges along the way, and I believe that people generally love to hear others talk about these things as well. Perhaps subconsciously,

as we listen to an interview with someone talking about these things, I think we all sort of wonder, "I wonder what I would do if I was in that person's shoes."

A couple years ago I came up with a tagline for my work in the PR field – *"Connect, Communicate, Change The World."* A lot of people might say, "Oh, my gosh, that's so idealistic! Are you kidding me? Aren't you interested in working with PR clients who just want to sell widgets or something like that?" I really do love working with people who help others through education or personal trans-formation, and that kind of thing. As a result, it wasn't that big a jump for me to move from working as a news producer to working in public relations. Like I said, I think of myself as a storyteller. When I was working on the news side of things, I was called upon to be a storyteller who paid meticulous attention to facts and details, and held back on giving anyone a rave review for a commercial product, because it would be inappropriate to violate the journalistic code of being neutral and objective. But even here on the PR side of things, where my job is to put the best face forward for my clients and really get them out there, this still has to be done with integrity. I think that when somebody really has a great story and it sparks the curiosity of viewers, listeners or readers, the person getting that amount of free airtime really deserves it. Some people in the PR field call that concept "earned media." It has to be a story that's strong enough to deserve a few minutes of airtime, and the audience watching or listening to the story has to be able to get something out of it.

Brian: I agree. One of the first guests we had on *The Business Experience Show* was a woman who had moved here from Vietnam. She owned and opened a number of nail salons, and I thought there was a lot to learn from her story. She had perfected her craft and had opened these nail salons in three different cities. It was the chosen profession that she created for herself, and she was able to successfully repeat the process of opening one nail salon after another. I think you'll find this kind of story in many different fields, and I think it's fascinating.

Tom: Exactly. I think that one of the biggest mistakes people can make is to say, "I'm just not going to listen to that person. There's nothing I could possibly learn from that person." They're basically "judging a book by its cover." Certainly, when I travelled America for Charles Kuralt at CBS "Sunday Morning," I interviewed a number of back woods farmers and fishermen and others from very humble professions. You might find yourself thinking, "What could this person possibly have to say that would be of value to my life?" I believe, however, that everyone really does have a story and a message worth listening to. I sometimes think that listening has become almost a "lost art."

Lisa: I think we share the same synergy in the way that we approach people, with a desire to discover their competitive advantages even if they seem to have lost sight of that part of the story themselves. It sounds like you're able to pull that kind of information out of them, by listening to them -- and even they're not unique in their industry, you're able to find their personal story, which really is unique. Can you explain the value of public relations, and of having a PR firm work with them? I would imagine that some people simply feel that they don't want to pay for PR support, right?

Tom: That's true, of course. I sometimes speak to groups about this topic, and I title my talk, "Do-It-Yourself Public Relations." In order to be successful with a public relations campaign -- and secure coverage in the newspaper or on the airwaves and so on -- like you said, a business or individual needs to have a distinct advantage. I ask them "Why are you special? Why do you stand out from the crowd?" I've handled PR for a number of financial advisors, for example. You might ask, "Aren't they all really interchangeable?" To be successful in helping one of those financial advisors get their story out there to a wider audience, you need to learn why that individual is unique. Some financial advisors are passionate about children's financial education, some are concerned with helping teachers prepare for their retirement, and so on. To help one of those individuals, I need to learn what's special and

unique about them. They might not be absolutely unique from every other financial advisor in the world, but at least you try to move in that direction.

There are different facets to the public relations process. You need to be able to connect with journalists who are "the gate-keepers" who can put a story on the air and share that story with the public. You need to be able to "speak the same language" as those journalists, so they can understand – in a very succinct way -- why the story idea is timely, and why it's newsworthy.

Also, there's one essential part of the process that I learned from the executive producer of "Good Morning America," when I was producing stories for that show. Every afternoon, the GMA staff would have our show meeting to make sure everything was lined up for the show the following morning. That daily meeting was also our chance to present new ideas for future shows. Every time a new story idea was mentioned, and every time one of the producers spoke about a story that was scheduled for the show the following morning, our executive producer Shelley

Ross always reminded us that our audience would be sitting at home asking one question, *"What's in it for me?"*

Working in the field of public relations, whenever I think about a story or a message, I find that there are "two sides to the same coin." On one side, when it comes to connecting with an audience and sharing a message, you have to be passionate. People are really drawn to those who are passionate about what they do. At the same time, however, you can't lose sight of genuinely serving that audience out there. If you're just dying to get on the air, and your intention is to use that time in a very self-serving way, simply talking about all the awards you've won, the history of your company, and so on, you're not really going to connect with your audience. If that's all you're doing, simply talking about yourself and losing sight of how you can serve the audience, I think that's a mistake and you're losing the opportunity to connect. In fact, you may be doing more harm than good. If you do make a genuine connection with your audience – by focusing on serving them, and delivering

value that will help them in their lives – I've found that this kind of connection really does result in sales and the growth of a business.

Brian: Do you have difficulty getting your clients to see the PR process that way? Everyone has their own vision of how their story should be told. You're saying that they have to focus on serving the audience and giving value, and not simply talking about themselves. Do people understand why this approach is necessary, and do they see the benefits of telling their story this way?

Tom: That's a very good question, of course. Human nature covers quite a broad spectrum, and not everyone is going to see the advantage of approaching the PR process in the way I just described, but many clients I've worked with do see it this way. When I was first starting out in the PR business, whenever I met with someone who really felt compelled to tell the world how wonderful they were, in a very "self-absorbed" way, I often kept my opinion to myself. These days, however, I feel much more comfortable telling

Public Relations

people like this that a "self-absorbed" message like this simply is not going to resonate with the public, and will not result in the increased sales or attention they're seeking. As you suggest, however, not everyone wants to hear this. Also, I believe that the best clients – or at least the ones I prefer to work with -- are those who are patient and know that public relations is a process, just like internet marketing, website design, Search Engine Optimization, and so on. You don't get great results in a day. It's a matter of developing a strategy.

Lisa: Building your brand.

Tom: Exactly. It does take time. From what I've seen over the years, when it comes to responding to a pitch or story idea, every journalist has his or her own pace. Some people are going to jump on a story as soon as you suggest it, even if it's just sort of a useful, interesting topic, and not something urgent that's going to dramatically change the world. A breaking news story has its own built-in urgency, of course. On the other hand, if a story idea seems useful and interesting but not urgent, some

producers and reporters will respond to your pitch by saying, "Well, that's an interesting idea. I'm going to put this in my file." Then, you may not hear from them again for three months. Another journalist may respond to the same pitch by saying, "Oh, my gosh! I was thinking about this exact subject today. You've read my mind! Can your client be on our show tomorrow?" Knowing that different producers will respond differently in this way, my approach is to cast a wide net because every one of the journalists I'm pitching has their own pace, and you really don't know what factors they're dealing with that might stand in the way of the story getting on the air – or, on the other extreme, help expedite the process. It may sound a bit silly, but one of the most useful lessons that I've learned from working in the PR field for so many years is to "never speculate" why something is or is not happening, in terms of a journalist responding to a pitch. There could be a million reasons why they're not responding or getting on board with a pitch that I think would make for a great story. To compensate for this, I always try to be as strategic as possible.

Lisa: Can you give us an example of someone you've worked with who was "a nobody," per se, who was willing to be patient in building the brand and building the story, who found that the PR process you just described worked well for them?

Tom: Sure. One example of someone I've worked with who was willing to be patient and trust in the process – although I certainly wouldn't call him "a nobody" – is my friend Ken Tencer, who is an author, and a branding and marketing consultant. Ken is a business innovation expert, based in Toronto. A couple years ago, Ken and his business partner John Paulo Cardoso wrote a book called *The 90% Rule*. It was a self-published book, telling readers that you don't need to be a giant firm like Apple to make innovation a steady ongoing part of how you do business. Aside from his clients, of course, Ken was relatively unknown – and had received little or no media attention. He wanted to become known as the voice of innovation – or at least a prominent and widely recognized expert in this field. As you may have noticed, especially if you happen to read *Entrepreneur*, *Fast Company*, or magazines like that on a regular basis, the topic of innovation has become somewhat of a crowded field these days, with a lot of people putting forward advice on that topic.

By connecting with radio hosts and producers, bloggers, podcasters, and a wide variety of financial and business journalists, and also by keeping our eyes open for stories in the news that Ken could add his expertise to, we began to let these "gate-keepers" know that Ken was someone worth talking to. We began to secure a variety of radio, television, and online spots, and as our work together proceeded, Ken's local newspaper in Toronto, The Globe and Mail, gave him a spot as a regular contributor, focusing on innovation. Again, it was just a matter of making sure that Ken made himself useful.

If you're an expert on Internet marketing or career advice, or whatever your specialty may be, notice how you might be

Public Relations

able to serve your local news outlets. When I was working at "Good Morning America," for example, I'd spend three or four hours a day trying to get a hold of certain experts who could provide the sound bites for whatever story I happened to be working on that day. We had a story in mind we wanted to tell, but we needed experts to share their opinions for each story. For that reason, if you just look for the appropriate media outlets that might be interested in your expertise or product, and let them know you're available, it can lead to some nice coverage. (Don't forget that journalists are "working people just like you and me," which means that if you can fill a useful spot in the story they're working on that day, there's a greater chance they can get home an hour or two earlier than might otherwise be possible. For the same reason, if you happen to catch a journalist on the phone, I recommend keeping your pitch to 30-seconds, rather than an hour!)

Over the course of two or three years, my friend Ken developed a very busy "In the News" page for his website. After being featured in numerous interviews and articles, whenever a potential customer looked at Ken's website, they said, "Oh, my gosh, he's been interviewed 50 times, all over the place!" That really is very persuasive, in terms of connecting with new clients and customers. Because of the way Ken has been able to expand his "brand aware-ness," so to speak, he has been able to raise his fees and he has been hired as a speaker at a number of high profile conferences, including the "World Innovation Conven-tion" in Cannes, France, where he has been invited to lead a workshop several times. As you can see, PR has really helped my friend Ken, and positioned him as an expert, because when you're inter-viewed on a news program or featured in a magazine or newspaper, that's really a priceless "stamp of credibility." Yes, you can buy an ad, but if a journalist says, "This person is worth listening to," that just separates the person from the pack. In this sense, PR can be very valuable.

There are many professionals who would love this kind of recognition and visibility, of course, but many of them think they're going to get there, "from zero to 60" immediately, and they don't understand that it's a process and takes time. The key to this kind of recognition is being useful to a wide audience. I encourage people seeking this kind of visibility to look for the media outlets that are a good fit for them, and let the journalists who write for these outlets, or who produce for these shows, know what they have to offer. I also believe, as I said earlier, that if somebody want to get some air time and just wants to talk about the awards they've won and how great they are – in short, they want to indulge in a bit of "an ego trip" – I think they're going to be disappointed. Everyone who works hard and offers customers a superior product or service is entitled to be proud of themselves, but let's not forget about really serving the audience. I encourage people to ask themselves, *"How can I be of service? How can I help people?"* Many times, I'll encourage my clients to offer free advice whenever they do an interview with the media. I believe this is useful advice, even for experts who work in highly specialized fields like "brain surgery" or "rocket science," fields in which it really seems like people need to hire that expert in order to benefit from their talent and expertise. I would still encourage them to think of a way to give people some tips or insights or advice with respect to their field, or help them see their field in a new way.

Every once in a while, I'll come across an interview with an author who responds to a question by saying, "The answer to that question is in chapter six of my book, which is now available for purchase at bookstores everywhere." That's the worst thing that someone can do in an interview situation. By sharing information and advice freely with an audience, with "no strings attached," they will automatically say, "Oh my gosh, that person is a great expert!" Then, they'll have a natural desire to see how they might keep this connection moving forward – perhaps by hiring this expert to help them.

Also, in a situation like this, the power of reciprocation kicks in, because people are naturally appreciative of those who help them or who freely share beneficial information. When they see someone positioned as an expert in this way, they naturally begin to ask themselves, "How can I help this person in return?" They also give some thought to hiring this person for their expertise. I really think it works this way.

Lisa: I agree with you, Tom. I think it can be very valuable to show people how you can be of service to them. I've done educational workshops where I've shown an audience of people what this means visually. I show a photograph of someone who is the number one mortgage broker in the whole country holding his or her "humongous" gold trophy. And no one in the audience – whether it's an audience of fifty people or 500 people -- responds to that. The person with that trophy is clearly self-absorbed, and is telling the world, "Look how wonderful I am!" Then I'll show the audience a picture of that same person hugging an old lady. Perhaps this mortgage broker helped the lady sell her home. Everyone's response to this photo is a harmonious, "Aww!" It's wonderful to be number one in your industry, but people don't really care about that. (Remember, Avis Rental Car had a very successful advertising campaign for many years, featuring the tag line "We're number two, we try harder!") In other words, the audience is saying, "Show me, your potential customer, how you are going to help me, not sell me."

Tom: That's an excellent point – and that reminds me that when doing an interview, telling stories and "painting a picture" are so important. For a number of years, I worked with the national management team of Feeding America, the nation's largest non-profit food bank organization, helping them with media training – and this is advice that I shared with them. For a number of years, the organization's CEO was a wonderful lady who had been a top executive for Delta Airlines before moving over to lead Feeding America. She's a very caring person, and very dedicated to helping those in need. Because of her corporate background, however, when responding to questions, she often focused on impressive and alarming statistics about the state of hunger in America. One of the most helpful things I did, in our media training sessions, in my opinion, was to tell her, "What you really need to do when you're interviewed is to tell stories, and 'paint a picture.'"

I asked her, "When you visit these different food banks around the country, what do you notice?" And she replied, "I notice that about ten percent of the hungry people showing up for food at these food banks are children, and that really breaks my heart." I said, "Well, I think you should talk about that. Is there a certain moment, a certain experience that really touched you, regarding the children you've met that various food banks?" And she said, "Yes. One time in Minnesota, I saw a little girl in a food line take a sandwich from the tray. She ate half the sandwich, and put the other half in her pocket. So I knelt down and said to her, 'What's the matter, honey, aren't you hungry today?' And she said, 'Oh yes, ma'am, I'm very hungry, but I'm bringing the other half of this sandwich home for my little sister, who hasn't eaten in two days." When you "paint a picture" like that during a television interview, viewers will say, "Wow! I really want to make a contribution to Feeding America." This kind of thing really generates a picture in the mind of each viewer – and, more importantly, it triggers powerful emotions. I really believe that telling stories and painting a picture in this way can be very powerful.

Brian: Do you ever handle public relations situations that you might consider "crisis PR," relating to some kind of emergency? In the news, we often see reports about various crisis situations, where a company or individual can really benefit from the help of a skilled PR person. Have you handled any situations like this?

Tom: I've been working with Scarlett Lewis, a mother in Newtown, Connecticut, which is pretty close to where I live. Scarlett's six year old son Jesse was killed in the Newtown tragedy in December 2012. It's really disturbing how many times we hear news stories about yet another school shooting, and Scarlett is often called on like so many people who have been touched by tragedy. Many people like Scarlett who have been touched by tragedy naturally want to make a difference in the world,

Public Relations

and when a similar story unexpectedly happens in the news, she has often wanted to see how she can help or provide the perspective of someone who has been through a similar situation. I work with breaking news in that sense, and I've also worked with a number of companies, coaching them on how to handle unexpected negative attention, which can often pop up when you least expect it. It's wise to be prepared in advance, in case they ever need to respond to an emergency. Also, I think we've all seen various news stories involving a company, when the company seems to take a very long time to speak out publicly about the situation. I believe this is always a big mistake.

Lisa: You've given our readers some good information on the importance of public relations. Thanks for your time. I'm sure that the information you've shared with us will help many people, Tom.

Tom: Thanks for this opportunity, Brian and Lisa!

Build Your Own Dream
Or Someone Else
Will Hire You
To Build Theirs

The Power Of Asking

I met Donald Trump at an event around 2006 from a radio promotional event. At the time, 97.1 FREE FM gave huge parties to the top advertisers and shows. Donald Trump attended and he was saying no to everyone who was asking for a photo with him. Little does he know that I do not take no for an answer.

With that in mind, I had a friend with me who I told, "Get your camera ready. Watch, I will ask him. He'll say yes and we'll be ready." I approached him with a big smile, nodding my head up and down and said the word "Picture?"

He couldn't say no, because my head was nodding yes. Click, click. After that, everyone else started asking for photos all because I got him to say yes.

Public Relations

Radio Interviews

If you've got a business or message to promote, giving a great radio interview with media training is an effective, easy, and free way to share your ideas with a wide listening audience. Doing a radio interview is especially convenient because you can "phone it in." There's no need to even leave the office. The host can record the entire conversation over the phone for later playback. But with the prevalence of podcasts, mp3 players, and all manner of on-demand media just a click or a tap away, many business executives may wonder if radio is even relevant anymore. The answer is yes! Radio listeners not only exist in our media-saturated world, but they are a dedicated and loyal audience who will listen to what you have to say.

5 Tips For Giving A Memorable Radio, Video, Or Media Interview

When giving a radio interview, you want to come across as well-informed and well-spoken, and that does not happen by accident. Before you get ready for your next radio interview, consider the following five tips to help you put your best self out on the airwaves.

1. Prepare With A Goal In Mind

Preparation is the key to a successful interview. You do not want to go in cold! Instead, try to come up with a goal:

What's your message you want the listener to take away for the interview?

How will you inform listeners to take "next steps" in line with what you are talking about?

What action do you want them to take after they hear you on the air?

Answering these questions as you prepare will keep your thoughts more focused. It is also a good idea to anticipate the questions you may be asked and have answers ready for them. This is not to say that you should write a word-for-word script, as that will almost certainly make you sound too rehearsed and unnatural. Keep *flash cards* and practice them in advance. Practice them with a friend so that you know how to respond to a question. I call these "sound bites" or "snippets of information." As essential as they are, you should refer to them often, as no one listening will see you checking them, but with enough practice you will know them from heart.

2. Eyes And Ears Are Everywhere

It is essential to remember that everything you say in a radio interview can stay with you and remain associated with you and your business. You want to be positive and honest. Speak accurately and truthfully, and if you cannot give a valid response to an interviewer's question, say so, with a promise that you will get back to him or her with a proper answer. Be genuine. It is okay to laugh and enjoy your interview just as if you would a conversation. Engage with the host and be willing to ask your questions to them, relative to the topics. This is another great reason to be prepared, as speaking off the cuff can cause you to make some erroneous remarks that can have negative implications down the road.

3. Keep To The Point

While it may seem that the interviewer has the control over your conversation, you have actually got quite a bit of power in direction the interview takes. If the line of questions starts to veer off into uncomfortable territory, bring it back to your more positive talking points. If you know that the interview will be edited before it airs, you can even ask for a few minutes to look over your notes and get your thoughts together. If it is recorded live, however, do your best to segue back to the message you want to promote. Remember, no matter what the interviewer asks, you are in control over what you say. If it appears that the person asking the questions has an ulterior motive, do your best to stay calm and gracious, and you will always come across well.

4. Practice The Art Of The Transition

Part of keeping control of a radio interview is learning the subtle yet effective practice of transitioning from an uncomfortable topic to a more positive one. Transitioning is not ignoring a question or giving a

Public Relations

response that does not answer what the interviewer asked. Rather, it is offering a simple, succinct answer to the question, and then using a transitional phrase to bridge back to your message. For example, after answering the original question, you might say something like, "I would also like to add," "To put that in perspective," or "One thing I would like listeners to remember is," and then connect it to what you came on the air to discuss.

5. Make It Memorable

Consider your audience as you prepare for your radio interview. What do you want them to come away with after listening to your conversation with the host? As you prepare notes for your interview, these take-away points are good places to start. Come up with a few, and then develop a strategy to convey them to your audience. It is also not a bad idea to reiterate these take-away items at the end of an interview. A host will often ask his or her guests if there is anything else the audience should hear about; that is the perfect time to go over your bullet points.

Finally, be sure to thank the radio host and producer off air. Take the time to mail a handwritten note card, and if they have not received your book or sample product – mail it to them.

CHAPTER 19:
Conclusion

It's simple:

- I want you to get found.
- I want your customers to find you more customers because you did a great job!
- I want you to get more business…and…make more money!

It does not matter who you are or what your business is. There is a full palette of colorful tools that can help your business grow.

And it all comes down to refining and distributing your message!

Conclusion

A while back I was jogging in my neighborhood when I saw a girl with a lemonade stand. *I can't help it* – I immediately looked at the marketing aspect of her stand. I grabbed her business card and read: *babysitter & dog walker*. What stood out besides her ambition was that her card was printed on a piece of paper – a homemade card.

I said, "People will tell you to get real business cards made, but ignore them. These cards are perfect for you and for people to want to help you.

As we left, my running partner said "I saw the lemonade, but you saw something completely different. I had not even noticed the business cards, but you were right, they were perfect for HER business and drew the right kind of attention." I also went on to hire her.

What I have come to learn in all these years of writing messages for people and brands – everything starts with writing…..words. Creativity comes second. All the other tools and 360 degree strategy is developed around your messages. I want you to choose the right ones or go back to the drawing board and have someone help you. Bounce ideas off those you trust. Be open to critique and change.

The best time to plant a seed was twenty years ago. The second best time is now! – Chinese Proverb

Conclusion

Please don't be like a stale seasoned business owner, who I often come across, who have been in business 25+ years. They are not quick to be innovative. It drives me crazy.

"Your success makes you blind to new ways of thinking," is a response I have to such staleness.

Stay innovative. Remain influential. Be purposeful.

I wish you the best of luck in your journey ahead!

RECOMMENDED LINKS AND TALKS

Popular Links And Radio Show Talks

5 Biggest Mistakes People Make When Starting A Business
by Phil Ehrlich, New York Attorney
Listen at: http://tinyurl.com/posel5t

The host of *The Tom Leykis Show* talks about his hiatus, entrepreneurship, technology, and marketing.
Interview with Tom Leykis, Radio Host
Listen at http://tinyurl.com/my2r4fb

16 Traits Of The World's Most Successful People
by Richard Feloni, *Business Insider* via Entreprenur.com
Read at http://www.entrepreneur.com/article/236554

Our business team trades jabs for a full hour with one of the fiercest fighters on the planet as *The Business Experience Show* gets professional heavyweight boxer David "El Nino" Rodriguez (36-0, 34 KOs) in the studio to discuss business plans, marketing strategies, and future goals. Our think tank gives him a business workout in our training camp for entrepreneurs. And the charismatic, sports entertainer comes through like a true champion. This show is great for anyone interested in sports or business.
Interview with Professional Heavyweight Boxer David Rodriguez
Listen at http://tinyurl.com/lpk2td4

Teen Entrepreneurship. "It's never too early to teach teens business."
Interview with Dean Stephen Christensen, Dean of the School of Business, Concordia University
Listen at http://youtu.be/iBkBX-o9iuk

Author John Cecil knows a lot about video and the future of Internet commerce. That is why he wrote the new book *Online Video Revolution: How To Reinvent And Market Your Business Using Video*.
Interview with John Cecil
Listen at http://tinyurl.com/pno4mmq

The Importance of Blogging
by Blogger Ashley Torres
Living a double life as CPA by day and blogger by night, Ashley Torres made the remarkable shift from passionately pursuing a hobby to launching a dream career via her blog *Life, Love, and the Pursuit Of Shoes*.
Listen at: http://tinyurl.com/kjr3rlt

The author of *The 90% Rule* and *Cause A Disturbance* talks about identifying business opportunities and how to pursue them effectively.
Interview with Author Ken Tencer
Listen at http://tinyurl.com/np255h5

Businesses can crowd source their creative services such as graphic design, business card design, stationery, web design, company names, product names, slogans, taglines, and writing projects.
Listen at http://tinyurl.com/muysy4s

He has reigned as one of daytime TV's sexiest bad boys since the 90's on *General Hospital*, *The Bold & The Beautiful*, and *The Young & The Restless*. All while juggling Hollywood feature films as an actor, producer, and writer. Sean Kanan visits our studio to talk about life in show business.
Interview with Actor Sean Kanan
Listen at http://tinyurl.com/mllzv2v

The revolutionary customer service techniques detailed in *The Renegade Server* apply to many industries. The often belittled food service industry does a 180° turn as this Harvard educated author, consultant, and speaker explains why being a waiter is the greatest entrepreneurial opportunity in America and how to make it so.
Interview with Tim Kirkland, Hospitality Expert and Author
Listen at http://tinyurl.com/ktjrsov

A discussion about business and estate planning, common scenarios, and basic planning strategies. Also the emotional impact on surviving family members of improper preparation.
Interview with Ted Hankin, Attorney and CPA
Listen at http://tinyurl.com/khpnx2r

Civil litigation attorney John Messina of Lytton Williams Messina & Hankin reveals his unlikely career path, the gamesmanship of the legal process, and the importance of careful contractual pre-planning. Listen at http://tinyurl.com/mr4u6n2

Feature film and commercial director Frank Lin makes a connection whether telling a warm family story or scaring the heck out of you. Learn about the business side of independent filmmaking from his stories on *The Business Experience Show*. Listen at http://tinyurl.com/oekdtgu

Photographer Michael Helms talks about making a living behind the camera. After 37 years as a Los Angeles photographer, he captures the perfect image through lighting, timing, and the perfect touch. Lighting and shooting are only 10% of the business. Making the subject comfortable, accenting the positive, influencing decision-makers, and navigating online marketing is where the real talent lies. Listen at http://tinyurl.com/nxzmccr

Financial Planning Tips from Scot Shier. Learn more about the financial services industry from investment and insurance strategist Scot Shier. We discuss investment strategy, business opportunity, financial protection. http://tinyurl.com/pdgwmkz

Vietnamese born Amanda Bui discusses owning nail salons in three different parts of the country. You will soon discover that business is a universal language with this compelling interview with Irvine California based Nails Paradise. Listen at http://tinyurl.com/ke43rc2

15 Signs You're an Entrepreneur By Marcia Layton Turner: http://m.entrepreneur.com/article/235378

Your smile is your logo,
Your personality is your business card,
How you leave other feeling
after having an experience
With you becomes your trademark.

SOURCES / CITATIONS / MENTIONS

"America Is Changing - National Conference of State Legislatures"
The Changing Face of America 1960-2050 (Slide)
Pew Research Center, Washington, DC
(August 15, 2013) Accessed August 20, 2014
http://www.ncsl.org/documents/summit/summit2013/online-
resources/taylorncsl2013.pdf

"Apps Solidify Leadership Six Years into the Mobile Revolution"
http://www.flurry.com/bid/109749/Apps-Solidify-Leadership-Six-
Years-into-the-Mobile-Revolution#.U9cXjoBdUxo

"Who Uses Social Networking Sites" (Social Networking Fact Sheet)
Pew Research Center, Washington, DC
(January 2014) Accessed on August 18, 2014
http://www.pewinternet.org/fact-sheets/social-networking-fact-sheet

"What is Your Simple, Repeatable Statement of Value?"
Maribeth Kuzmeski @RedZoneMarketer
(May 6, 2014) Accessed on August 19, 2014
https://www.linkedin.com/today/post/article/20140506110024-
915357-what-is-your-simple-repeatable-statement-of-value?trk=prof-
post

"Why your website is more important than social media."
Aaron Doucette. Marketing, Advertising, & Web Design @thisisapd
http://www.AaronDoucette.com/blog

"The Next America: Two Dramas in Slow Motion"
Percent of Population in US by Age Group (1950, 2015 & 2060)
Paul Taylor
(April 10, 2014) Accessed on August 18, 2014
http://www.pewresearch.org/next-america/#Two-Dramas-in-Slow-
Motion

SOURCES / CITATIONS / MENTIONS

"Millennials in Adulthood."
Pew Research Center, Washington, DC
(March 7, 2014) Accessed on August 15, 2014
http://www.pewsocialtrends.org/2014/03/07/millennials-in-adulthood

"Cell Phone Activities 2013"
Maeve Duggan
Pew Research Center, Washington, DC
(September 19, 2013) Accessed on August 18, 2014
http://www.pewinternet.org/2013/09/19/cell-phone-activities-2013

"The One Reason I Still Use Facebook"
David Keyes
https://www.linkedin.com/pulse/article/20140929190800-21677256-
the-one-reason-i-still-use-facebook-and-why-it-s-worth-20-billion

"Henry Ford Didn't Listen To His Customers and Facebook Shouldn't
Either."
Jennifer Grigg. (www.Twitter.com/TheSocialDragon)
Accessed on August 18, 2014
https://www.linkedin.com/pulse/article/20140730003452-131145214-
henry-ford-didn-t-listen-to-his-customers-and-facebook-shouldn-t-
either

"10 Ways to Establish Yourself (or Your Brand) as a Thought Leader"
DrewAHendricks. @DrewAHendricks
http://www.inc.com/drew-hendricks/10-ways-to-establish-yourself-or-
brand-as-a-thought-leader.html

"7 Reasons Why Innovation is Important"
Steven B. Johnson
via YouTube and http://wp.me/p2BAqb-pv

"Most Social Networks are Now Mobile-First"
http://www.statista.com/chart/2109/time-spent-on-social-networks-by-
platform

89382619R00109

Made in the USA
San Bernardino, CA
24 September 2018